The Unmaking
of the
American Working Class

ALSO BY REG THERIAULT

How to Tell When You're Tired: A Brief Examination of Work

The Unmaking
of the
American Working Class

Reg Theriault

THE NEW PRESS
NEW YORK

Published in the United States by The New Press, New York, 2003
Distributed by W. W. Norton & Company, Inc., New York

LIBRARY OF CONGRESS CATALOGING-IN-PUBLICATION DATA

Theriault, Reg, 1924–
    The unmaking of the American working class / Reg Theriault.
        p. cm.
    ISBN 1-56584-762-8 (hc.)
    1. Working class—United States.   2. Working class—United States—
Attitudes.   3. Blue collar workers—United States.   4. Work ethic—
United States.   5. Labor—United States.   I. Title.

HD8072.5 .T48   2003

305.5'62'0973—dc21   2002141416

The New Press was established in 1990 as a not-for-profit alternative to the large,
commercial publishing houses currently dominating the book publishing industry.
The New Press operates in the public interest rather than for private gain, and is
committed to publishing, in innovative ways, works of educational, cultural, and
community value that are often deemed insufficiently profitable.

The New Press, 450 West 41st Street, 6th floor, New York, NY 10036
www.thenewpress.com

Printed in the United States of America

10   9   8   7   6   5   4   3   2   1

Contents

CONTENTS

Prologue

In October of last year a Chinese ship from Shanghai appeared outside the Golden Gate. Aboard the vessel, as deck cargo, were four very large container cranes destined for a new container yard in Oakland where they would be used to load and discharge seagoing vans from ships calling at that Port. The booms of these new cranes, when laid flat with a container in their grasp, are so huge that they can span the largest of container ships and load sixteen rows, side by side, of eight-foot-wide seagoing vans. The cranes are so tall that the vessel transporting them had to heave-to and swing on its anchor while waiting for a very low minus tide so it could sail under and clear the Golden Gate Bridge.

Container cranes are, so to speak, indigenous to the San Francisco Bay Area. The very first container crane in the world was built in Oakland and began hoisting seagoing vans aboard ships in Alameda in 1959.

After the Chinese vessel from Shanghai passed through the Golden Gate, it docked in Oakland to discharge its cargo of container cranes. To everyone's surprise a crew of Chinese workers swarmed ashore and began setting up the cranes, readying them for use. This work is normally done by the Bridge Builders and Iron Worker's Union in the Bay Area, who protested this violation of their jurisdiction and the taking over of their work. Their objections came to nothing. It was subsequently discovered that these Chinese workers were laboring in America for four dollars a day.

Foreword

My mother and father, like most of the American working class of the past century, especially for those having lived through the Great Depression of the 1930s, hoped for a better life for their children than the one they looked back on. They saw the fulfillment of their hopes in education, getting their kids the education they never had. In a sense, of course, they were right. Statistics prove conclusively that there is a direct relationship between the number of years spent in school and one's income in later life. Other consequences of their efforts, however, were lost to them. For instance, greater income does not necessarily result in fewer everyday problems and a happier life. Furthermore, guiding your sons and daughters into the white-collar middle class, which is where education inevitably leads them, is an explicit put-down of your own blue-collar life and the values it embodies. For example, my mother despised middle-class attitudes while at the same time urging me toward a career that, if I were to be successful, I would have to embrace.

Inevitably, then, I went to college, specifically to matriculate in the study of some kind of engineering, a course my mother vaguely identified as leading to good opportunities and a better income. Unfortunately, it was one for which my preparation was utterly lacking. We were fruit-tramps, itinerant migratory workers. I changed school sometimes every three weeks. I never, for openers, ever systematically mastered long division, since the classroom I left was just beginning its study and, after moving on, the one I entered was just finishing it and beginning to delve into fractions. The end result of this was that later in college I flunked, all in one semester, physics, math, and chemistry. I later returned to a university, but to enroll in English literature. Hell, I liked to read.

Exposure as an adult to environments different than the one I had known as a child inevitably led me to examine and compare the white-collar to the blue-collar world. My conclusion resulted in my quitting the university, leaving Berkeley, and returning to the life of a fruit-tramp. I later became a longshoreman and spent a third of a century working on the San Francisco waterfront.

Returning to the blue-collar world was a move I have never regretted. However, as the years have gone by it has become more and more clear that our world, the world of hands-on blue-collar workers, is shrinking. Automation and factories fleeing overseas has reduced our work to the point that in many places in America it is almost nonexistent, leaving a void that has not and may never be filled. It is this loss of work and the life and ethic it engendered that prompted me to write this book. If there is a tragedy here, and I think there is, it lies in the fact that it did not have to happen. The fate of the American blue-collar worker could have been different.

*The Unmaking
of the
American Working Class*

CHAPTER ONE

On the Waterfront

On the first of June, 1959, I began working as a longshoreman on the San Francisco waterfront. Although not young—I was in my middle thirties and I had a wife and three sons—I turned-to at the pier that first day regarding the job as only temporary, like every other job I had held up to then. As it turned out I was to remain a working longshoreman for the next thirty-four years, until I retired and closed out my working life.

My people were fruit-tramps. I was born into that loose but very well-defined tribe of itinerant agricultural workers who, for almost a century, wandered the western United States working the crops, packing the fruits and vegetables which were shipped in refrigerated railroad cars to markets all over America.

What started out originally as essentially hobo's work had by the 1920s been institutionalized into an occupation in which several hundred families made a yearly living, traveling by automobile, of course, instead of riding the rails. By the time I reached adulthood the range of the western fruit-tramp had expanded to Arizona and even all the way down to the lower Rio Grande Valley of Texas, where the earliest spring melons in America were harvested. Phoenix and Yuma, Arizona, and the Imperial Valley of Southern California became big centers for growing summer cantaloupes and winter lettuce. I worked both commodities in these and other places, and, like most fruit-tramps, in a burst of freedom occasionally jumped from one job to another just for the hell of it.

My people came out of the Northwest, Washington state, as did most of the early fruit-tramps, and their old Wobbly attitudes from the anarchist creed of the International Workers of the World made them clannish toward outsiders, especially the boss. These attitudes remained with them as they spread south. When they found work they naturally sent word back to other fruit-tramps. Eventually, almost every packing shed in the western United States, its wages, its working conditions, and its ethics, was dominated by the fruit-tramp presence. No member of management gives up power over his workforce willingly, and most growers and shippers bitterly resented an intrusion by a crew of packers into areas of decision they considered theirs to make. The fruit-tramps, however, practiced restraint by and large, and, with time, many shippers came to respect us and our work. If we insisted on top wages, we worked long hours when needed to get the crop packed out. If we were touchy and temperamental at times, we transported ourselves from job to job at our own expense, and, most importantly, we did our work well. A properly packed crate of melons or a lug-box of tomatoes carefully sized and wrapped in tissue paper sold for top money when it arrived at market, something that home guards and cowboys were incapable of achieving.

Apples from the Northwest were the first commodity to be shipped in volume to the East, but in Southern California huge acreages of oranges groves were being planted that very quickly constituted winter work for our family after the fall apple crop had been wrapped up. After their first swing south my folks were hooked on California. There weren't just oranges; there was a lot of other stuff grown that paid good money for experienced packers, and one crop or another was coming off almost the year around. Every fall for a number of years after migrating to California the family made the annual trip back to the Northwest and my parents packed apples, but it finally became more of a pilgrimage to the past than a need to find work. It was simply a hell of a lot warmer and dryer in California, and the living was easier. I was seven years old when we made our last trip to Washington.

History finally caught up with the fruit-tramps and did away with them and the way they made their living. Western agriculture colleges, through genetic engineering, developed seeds that produced tomatoes, cantaloupes, and other fruits and vegetables so tough they could be tossed roughly into durable cardboard cartons and survive a hard, bumpy trip to market. Industrial agriculture—factories in the fields—finished the fruit-tramp off. The skill was taken out of packing and the packing shed disappeared. Instead of hauling everything into town to be processed, the cartons were packed in the fields and loaded into refrigerator cars wherever the railroad had a siding. A few fruit-tramps found work in the new harvesting process, but the growers and shippers preferred alien workers, mostly Mexicans. Mexicans worked cheaper, and if they got themselves organized and sought more money and better working conditions, which they frequently did, they could be rounded up, shipped back across the border, and replaced with new ones of a more docile nature.

Cantaloupes were the last of our work to go to the fields. Melons *are* fragile and require more skill and care in their handling, and fruit-tramps continued packing them long after they had lost their work in the other commodities. For years I eagerly waited for summer to come around again, for the jobs to start up, and my fruit-tramp life to begin once more. Winters, however, presented a problem in how to make a living. Finally, late one summer when the last cantaloupe had been packed, I settled my family in San Francisco and began to search again for a winter job. I chose San Francisco because the Bay Area was familiar to me, having attended four semesters at Berkeley when I got out of the army at the end of World War II. However, I was a firmly committed blue-collar worker and it was its industries that attracted me to the Bay Area. In those days you could find a job almost anywhere. As usual I planned to quit whatever job I had when summer rolled around and the melons started up again.

I worked two winters in two different factories, two more winters on the San Francisco produce market, and one winter in the post office loading sacks of mail onto trucks. In late spring when the melons began to ripen I quit whatever job I was working and took off south to fruit-tramp again. Sometimes I took the family with me; more often I went alone. It would not be accurate to say I disliked factory life—I genuinely liked most of my coworkers wherever I worked—but the absence of movement and change was more than I could handle. What I needed, I became aware, was a permanent job that incorporated the freedom and choice I knew as a fruit-tramp. After several years of batting around from one job to another every winter, I had almost given up hope of finding work I was happy with. And then, after having been closed for over ten years, the San Francisco waterfront opened up and hired new men. I became a longshoreman.

I think I had always had longshoring in the back of my mind as an alternative to fruit-tramping. To other workers in the western United States longshoremen on the West Coast had, since the knock-down-drag-out strikes of the mid-1930s, achieved a mythical, almost heroic status, much of it deserved. They had very good wages and just about the best working conditions one could find in any industry. And they did not take crap off of anyone, starting with the stevedore companies and shipping interests that employed them. West Coast longshoremen had a code of ethics and conduct similar to that of the fruit-tramps, both coming out of the Wobbly movement dating back to the early years of the century in the Pacific Northwest. But even among the fruit-tramps, who had their own heroes, longshoremen were the one group above all others who kept the faith of "an injury to one is an injury to all," and the most heinous of crimes was to scab during a strike.

Their union, the International Longshoremen and Warehouse Union, was headed by the famous (and to some infamous) Harry Bridges. It had been put together with muscle, democratic muscle, by maritime workers in the mid-1930s, starting with a wildcat strike in the spring of 1934 in San Francisco. The strike started in opposition to the "shape-up," a system of hiring by the stevedore bosses that permitted them to show favoritism to selected longshoremen. Early each morning the men gathered at whatever pier had a ship in. The boss would look over the mob of men, all hungry for work, and pick and choose whomever he decided he was going to use that morning. "Kickbacks" to the boss in the form of money from the men for the privilege of working that day were common.

What had started as a spontaneous work stoppage quickly spread up and down the West Coast until all the major deep-sea ports in western America were shut down. The ship owners responded with

5

National Guard troops, tear-gas, clubs, and rifle fire, leaving workers dead and maimed from San Pedro in Southern California to Seattle in the Northwest. With two men dead on the sidewalk in San Francisco and uncounted others bludgeoned senseless by cops and company goons along the waterfront, the teamsters and other workers joined the longshoremen and astounded established authority by expanding the wildcat work stoppage into a general strike, shutting down the entire city of San Francisco.

The general strike lasted four days, during which nothing moved without permission of the strike committees, who apportioned out food so no one went hungry and policed the city so effectively that crime, briefly, became nonexistent. Very quickly New Deal Washington under President Roosevelt initiated arbitration machinery, which finally resulted in longshoremen gaining control over how they worked. They set up hiring halls staffed by dispatchers elected from among their own rank and file, and effectively did away with favoritism and corruption.

Despite being under almost constant attack over the years by both the ship owners and the United States government, the International Longshore and Warehouse Union had survived and prospered until, by the time I joined it, the Union represented not only longshoremen in the three western states, but also in Canada and Alaska. In addition, there were ILWU members working in warehouses and plants extending as far inland as the center of the Mojave Desert. ILWU crewmen worked fish boats and ferries from San Diego to the Bering Sea. As a further triumph the entire Hawaiian archipelago was ILWU. Sugar-cane cutters and pineapple workers, both in the fields and in the canneries, and longshoremen there, too, of course, had been organized after a series of bitter strikes. They had prospered until Hawaii had the highest-paid agriculture workers in the world. In the Islands the ILWU was even beginning to organize the tourist industry. Everyone from busboys and chambermaids through chefs and waitresses were showing up wearing union buttons. The men and women of the ILWU could look back on an impressive list of accomplishments. Their successes had been due to their own blue-collar, rank-and-file efforts and, mostly, grass-roots leadership. We other workers were, quite frankly, somewhat in awe of them. Still, when I started working the docks that day in early June, I had in the back of my mind that I might take off again and fruit-tramp later in the summer.

I quickly realized that longshoremen were unlike any other group of workers I had ever known. Almost everyone, including most of the rank and file, were seriously caught up in politics, both in the union and the world outside. Every fall when the union elected its officers for the coming year there were several candidates for every position, from the president on down. City, state, and national politics received equally intense activity. Every congressional candidate came down to our union meetings and solicited our votes.

Left-wing orthodoxy of a rigid Stalinist kind was still maintained by a small but vocal group within the San Francisco local when I joined it. They, the ossified remnants of communists and fellow travelers left over from a once large and vital radical movement dating back to the thirties in the city, still had some influence within the union. I was a lefty, too, but my affinities were toward people like George Orwell and Albert Camus, politically at the opposite end of the spectrum from those holding power in the Soviet Union and their adherents in Local 10 in San Francisco. This group tolerated no opposition from other lefties. I had a couple of friends, long-established Frisco longshoremen, who were viciously attacked at union meetings when they protested some inconsequential resolu-

tion designed to do nothing more than support Russian foreign policy. I was a provisional longshoreman. I could be dismissed at any
time until I was advanced to full union membership. This meant I
had to hang dead and be prudent in my response whenever anything
of a political nature was discussed. It was not an easy thing to do for
someone who had come out of fruit-tramping, where free thought
and discourse were unlimited. The rank-and-file longshoremen,
however, did not give a damn what an individual's politics were. The
older men with whom I worked accepted me as soon as I learned
how to rig the ship's gear and do the work. And the work was a lot
like fruit-tramping; every few days you moved on to different cargo
at a different pier on a different ship.

We were the first new longshoremen in over ten years to come on
the waterfront and we new men went through a period with the old-
timers that was very similar to boot camp or basic training. The old-
timers were gruff with us, but I think most of them were secretly
glad to have some younger men around for a change. They got to tell
us what to do, pass on waterfront lore and work habits, and shake
their heads at us when we made mistakes. We also had to take their
ribbing and listen to their jokes, endlessly repeated until their telling
became a joke among us newcomers. Once during my first week on
the job while lashing down cargo on the deck of a ship, I ran into a
problem. The chain was too short. I could not get the shackle-pin
through to its opposite hole to secure the cargo to the steel deck. By
this time I was certainly aware that one could not stretch chain, but I
was trying anyway. No matter how hard I pulled, I could not take up
enough slack to get the pin through to its opposite hole. I had an old
Swede winch-driver looking over my shoulder.

"I'll bet," the old winch-driver commented, "that if that hole had
hair around it you wouldn't have any trouble finding it! Har, Har,

Har, Har!" He used that line on so many of us that, even years later, when someone inquired who the winch-driver was on some job and you replied, "Har, Har, Har," there was no need for further identification. In spite of the very hard work I grew to love the job. Summer was half over before I realized one day that it was getting late in the year; I had to choose one or the other, longshoring or fruit-tramping. It was really no choice at all; I had found a new home on the waterfront. I was a longshoreman. Years later I went back and fruit-tramped, but that was only to introduce my three sons to a life I had once known.

My first day at work, however, was numbing. I drew a job discharging sacks of coffee from the very bottom of the hold of a ship. A sack of coffee weighs 70 kilos, 154 pounds. We discharged twelve sacks to a load on a rope sling. My partner and I, one of three teams in a six-man gang working in rotation, had to be ready to meet the hook with a full sling-load of coffee every time it came back into the hold empty from the dock. And it always seemed to be our turn. At the end of the day I climbed the ladder out of the hatch dog-tired. When I drove home I sat in the car out in front of the house for twenty minutes, until my kids came out and helped me drag my weary bones up the stairs and into a hot bath. Apparently longshoring required the use of muscles that fruit-tramping had never developed in me.

CHAPTER TWO

How to Steal Sheep

My father was born in 1898 in a little town in west-central Washington state. In the West in those days male children of nonaffluent families were expected to be hard to raise. A boy got into mischief early, and serious, perhaps even criminal, trouble by his middle teens. And then he left home. Frequently he was farmed out to a relative in another locale, an uncle, perhaps, which sometimes worked out. An eighth-grade education was standard, if he made it that far. After that he was no longer a boy and was supposed to go to work. My father pretty much followed that pattern.

My mother was born in the same year as my father on a farm in central Wisconsin. Her education almost exactly duplicated that of my father: a rather steady attendance at school during the winter months, and then piecemeal learning during the spring and fall when farm work at home took precedence over everything else.

When she did attend classes, however, she must have paid attention; her handwriting was always better than my father's, and she wrote letters. His rare postcards to me contained little capitalization and almost no punctuation.

For boys not yet fully grown in my father's day, jobs were exploitative, ill paying, and usually short-lived. Although the apprentice system was still intact, small towns in western America simply had no factories or industry. In the Northwest, that left agriculture and timber, lumberjacking and the sawmill, or threshing wheat in eastern Washington; or, in the fall, working in the rapidly expanding apple orchards around the foothills of the Cascades.

I do not know what kind of trouble precipitated my father's first leaving the community into which he was born, or even his precise age. He never told me and I never asked. It was not a question that passed between my father and me. Actually my father never sat me down and told me anything. What I know of him when he was young I gathered early on by sitting quietly in corners and listening to adult conversation, and later, when grown, by sitting quietly on a bar stool and listening to him and his friends talk about the old days earlier in the century in the Northwest. I know that by his fifteenth birthday my father had already left home.

"Remember the sheep?" The question was asked by Bill Heine, a man my father's age whose friendship with him went back to those early days. It was late September, the first summer after World War II. I was just out of the army and we three, my father, Bill Heine, and I, were sitting in a dingy bar in a small San Joaquin Valley town in central California. We were winding up a cantaloupe deal, packing melons on a shed that had about three more days of work left to complete the harvest and then the cantaloupes would be over until next year. The pickers out in the country were still working on one last field for the day, so we packers knocked off work in the shed for an hour and a half to give them time to finish up and bring the last loads of melons into town. Where else do you go for an hour and a half in the middle of the afternoon except to a bar?

"What sheep?" my father asked.

"The sheep we stole for that sheriff in that little town near Yakima," Bill replied.

My father shrugged. Then he smiled. "You mean the sheep we were supposed to get a dollar apiece for?" he said.

Bill grinned and turned to me. "Used to be," he said, "up in Washington the sheep were brought down from the mountains in the fall of the year, just before the snows come. Those were big, big herds, strung out for miles on this narrow trail along the river. They'd have a man, one man, in the lead and another man, with a dog, usually, back maybe half a mile, bringing up the rear. This was a narrow trail where the sheep had to come along mostly in single file, but never more than two abreast. It was a twisty trail along the river, and at one point there was this old deserted building, a portage shed of some kind, on the bank extending down to the water. The sheep trail ran right in front of it. Our job—your dad and me—was to hide inside the shed until after the lead man had gone around the bend and before the tail-end man had yet to come into sight. Then, for a minute or two, we would run out and grab sheep. We'd drag them into the shed and drop them through a trap door into a cellar down below the main ground level. Those sheep would be coming along that trail all day long. We'd get four or five sheep out of each herd, wouldn't we, Doug?"

My father nodded. "I'm surprised we got away with it," he said. "Every time we grabbed an animal it would bleat holy hell. I still don't know why those sheepherders didn't get wise to us. They must have missed their animals when they took a count down below, but none of them ever came back looking for their lost sheep."

"Yeah, you're right, Doug," Bill said thoughtfully. "But maybe they did come back and we were long gone."

Bill had called my father Doug. Only my mother and a few others ever called my father Doug. Everyone else called him Don. He was one of those people who, over a lifetime, acquired several names. I once encountered a woman who called him Tony.

"How's Tony?" she asked.

"Tony who?" I responded.

"Tony, your father, for Christ's sake. Who else?"

"Oh, he's okay," I replied, trying to figure that one out. "He's running a lettuce job down in El Centro."

"The hell he is," she said. "The hell he is. Maybe I'll go down there and trim lettuce for him," she added, turning away.

"Why don't you," I said. "Tell him hello."

I found out where the Tony came from some years later when I applied for a passport. It wasn't a given name, but an abbreviation of a surname. At the time of my birth my father's last name was Anthony. I was an Anthony, or had been. I spent a big part of one summer in dingy bars in dusty Valley towns chasing down old fruit-tramps to get affidavits to prove to the State Department that I and Anthony were one and the same person.

Bill and my father had lapsed into silence. I was eager to hear more about the sheep, but I had learned it was wise not to press them too much. If they were inclined to do so they would talk about it in their own good time. Finally I gave up. "Where does the sheriff come in?" I asked.

"He recruited us out of jail," Bill said.

"What were you in jail for?" I asked my father.

He thought for a moment. "Nothing," he said.

"That sheriff was looking for a couple of kids like us," Bill said. "That's why we were in jail."

"A dollar a sheep," my father said, as if he were amused. "How many sheep did we steal over those three days, Bill?"

"We filled up that cellar three times," Bill said. "I never did figure out who those guys were that came and took them away each night."

"They were locals," my father said. "That sheriff had a ranch of his own somewhere back in the hills. The guys that took those sheep away were his guys. We were the only drifters. And we were the ones who were going to take the fall if anything went wrong. Five dollars," my father added.

"Yeah," Bill agreed. "A five-dollar goldpiece. One for each of us."

My father turned to me. "At the end of the third day we met that sheriff in town after dark. We thought we'd meet him in a bar, he'd pay us off, and we'd have a drink. Not that sheriff. He told us to meet him at the train depot. There in the dark he handed us each a five-dollar goldpiece. 'What's this?' I said. Bill and I figured we had a least a couple hundred bucks to split between us. 'That's it,' he said. 'That's all you get. Now,' he said, 'you see that freight train over there? That freight is leaving in five minutes. And you two better be on it or I'm arresting you both for stealing sheep.'" When my father spoke directly to me he was being instructional. My father picked up his beer and fell silent. Never trust a cop was the lesson this time. Hell, I already knew that. After a while Bill Heine spoke.

"Your old man wanted to punch him out," he said to me. "Can you imagine? Punching out a sheriff? I finally got Doug aboard that freight train."

From where we were sitting we could see the packing shed through the front window of the bar. There were supposed to be three loads left to come in from the field. When the second load pulled up to the dumping hamper we finished our beers and went back to work.

Packers worked off benches in those days, which they called humps, one behind another, all in a row. The melons were sorted into a bin on your right. You placed an empty crate on your hump from an overhead rack, and start grabbing melons. A wooden crate held anywhere from twenty-three to forty-five cantaloupes, according to size, the forty-fives being the smallest. When you finished filling the crate you set it off on a moving belt that took it away to the lidding machine. Cantaloupes had to be packed precisely by size into the crate, touching all the adjacent melons and fitting snugly against each other. If the melons were too loose, they would rattle around in the crate and destroy themselves in the refrigerator car on their trip to market. If they were packed too tight they would be crushed when they went through the lidding machine.

All work then was done on a piece-rate basis. When I started out packing we were getting ten cents a crate. It was important that the packer pack a good crate, but it was also equally important that he pack that crate fast. At the peak of the season the shed may be running from seven in the morning until after midnight. The packers, and all the rest of the shed crew including the sorters, the truckers, and loaders, were expected to hang in there and keep working. At the peak of the harvest the work went on into the night for as long as it took to get that day's harvest packed out. A packer was well paid. I was making six to eight dollars an hour when an average factory worker in America was making two, or even less. But I do not remember ever making a dollar I did not earn. In all other commodities—apples, pears, tomatoes, oranges—both men and women in approximately equal numbers were employed as packers. But a full crate of cantaloupes weighed in at eighty-five or ninety pounds so all the workers on a melon shed except for the checker, usually the boss's wife, were men. On that shed I packed right behind my father.

I packed cantaloupes behind my father several times, and when he ran jobs as shed boss, which he frequently did, I worked for him several other times. I could never beat my father at packing. He was simply faster than I was. If we started a crate at the same time he always set his off first. He would be reaching for an empty crate while I was still finishing my top layer. He would shake his head at me and tell me to speed it up. "They don't grow these things in winter," he might add. I once packed tomatoes right behind my mother, too, until I found an excuse to jump to another job. Tomatoes were wrapped, every one of them, in tissue paper. It helped preserve them when they were shipped somewhere east, like New York. About every third box of tomatoes I set off on the belt, my mother would stop packing and stare at it as it went by her. Then she would turn and give me her comment. "That last box you packed looked a little ragged."

"Yes, Mom."

Packing tomatoes was a vacation after packing cantaloupes all summer. The packing sheds were cleaner and a box full of tomatoes weighted only thirty-two pounds. Furthermore, most of the fall tomatoes in California were grown on the coast near the ocean where the cool breezes blow, a decided improvement over a stifling shed in the San Joaquin Valley where the August temperatures reached 110 degrees or more. We did not make as much money packing tomatoes. We were paid twelve cents a box and a good packer could set off only about twenty-five boxes an hour, which was still better than working on an assembly line. And there were other compensations. There were always several cute local girls working up on the sorting belt, not all of whom were unfriendly to a fruit-tramp.

CHAPTER THREE

The Union Makes Us Strong

The history of trade unions in America and the obstacles and opposition that workers had to overcome just to bring unions into existence are well documented. From the late nineteenth century onward, violence, or the threat of violence, to workers has always been present, even after the New Deal made belonging to a union an American right. Even when the threat of violence was less present, working people sometimes had to apply extreme ingenuity just to hold a meeting. I remember as a boy a gathering of fruit-tramps that took place on the bank of a river under a bridge in the pear country north of San Francisco. Since the river was a federal stream, it was, to its high-water mark, out of the jurisdiction of the local authorities who had repeatedly denied the shed workers a place to meet in town.

Although they were organized into a union in the early thirties, fruit-tramps rarely held general membership meetings. Scattered as they were over the entire West, the best their elected officials could hope for was regional attendance. Frequently they had difficulty getting anything done, or even maintaining control. In the instance of the meeting under the bridge, the fruit-tramps were about equally divided over what they wanted to do. Half of them wanted to return to the sheds in the morning and go out on strike for more money. The other half wanted to pull up stakes and leave. One packer put it succinctly, "I say we tell those damn farmers to pack their own goddamn pears. I'm heading south." With that he got up and left, taking half of those present with him. This Wobbly-style way of relating to the boss prevailed among the fruit-tramps even when strong, indigenous leadership came to the fore among them and channeled their energies toward the stability of industry-wide contracts—you got the same money for packing a crate of lettuce in Phoenix, finally, as you did in Salinas, California; seniority prevailed when someone was laid off; and all the packing sheds had to subscribe to the state unemployment fund so that everyone would have at least something to live on if they could not find a job in the winter.

Before I came to work on the waterfront I had been a member of two trade unions other than the fruit-tramp's, a small Teamster local and a nationally directed electrical worker's local dominated by the Communist Party. The electrical worker's union leadership took care of routine business matters rather well, but they and the employer's attitude toward each other was so adversarial that they could not come together to cooperate even on matters of common interest and mutual benefit. In the two years I belonged to it, the Teamster local never held a membership meeting, monthly dues were automatically withheld from our paycheck, and we never saw a business agent. Consequently, my first longshore union meeting was an eye-opener for me. For the first time I was to see a trade union functioning as an accepted part of the mainstream society in which it existed.

Longshore union meetings are held monthly and it is mandatory that members attend. One's union book is stamped at the meeting's end, and if you do not show evidence of attendance, you are fined at the end of the month when you pay your dues. This measure usually insures a pretty good turnout of the longshore rank and file.

In addition to Harry Bridges, the San Francisco longshoremen had, when I joined them, one other member of international renown, Eric Hoffer, the worker-philosopher. I had met Hoffer and I had read all his books, starting with *The True Believer,* but I did not know him. I had never met Harry Bridges. I had been told that both men were expected to be present at the meeting that night.

The meeting started promptly at seven o'clock. I came early and secured a good seat in the front row of the balcony where I could observe everything that was going on. The Local 10 president holding office for that year, an aging Irishman, called the meeting to order from the podium and asked the sergeant-at-arms to make a count to verify that there was a quorum present. The sergeant-at-arms, responding from one of the three microphones stationed down on the floor for the rank and file's use, stated that there was not a quorum present, but that there were at least twice as many members milling around outside in the parking lot as there were in the hall, and that if everyone would come inside then there would be a quorum well over. The president authorized the sergeant-at-arms to assemble a posse of sufficient size to accomplish the round up.

Seated on the stage behind the president was the secretary-treasurer at his own little table where he could record the minutes of the meeting. In a line of chairs behind the secretary were two business agents, the chief dispatcher, a trustee of the union, and a man dressed in an expensive suit whom I recognized as one of our Bay Area congressmen, up for reelection in the fall. While the men began flowing in from outside, the president turned to the member of the House of Representatives and asked him if he would like to say a few words to the assembled longshoremen. The congressman thanked the president, shook his hand, and leaned into the microphone.

The congressman cited a number of bills pending in Congress having to do with labor, which he intended to support, and an equal number which he, in conjunction with some of his colleagues, hoped to defeat. He timed his speech to end when the auditorium became full, thanked everyone for their attention, shook the president's hand again, and left. Before calling the meeting to order the president remarked that the congressman's hurried departure was due to the fact that he had three other union meetings to attend that evening before flying back to Washington on the Midnight Special. He added that the congressman had the wholehearted endorsement of the entire union.

When the president called the meeting to order, his first act was to ask everyone to stand and salute the flag, which prompted a small contingent of men in the first few front rows to remain defiantly seated. When the pledge was completed and those men standing began to sit down, a number of those who had remained seated leaped to their feet and lined up behind the three microphones down in front of the podium. This was the late fifties, the height of the Cold War, but I had no inkling of what was taking place.

The president called on everyone to stand again for a minute of silence—there were no dissidents this time—while the secretary read the names of three men, two of them retirees, who had died since the last meeting. When the reading of the agenda was completed, the man at the head of the line on the floor microphone on the left cleared his throat loudly. It reverberated from loudspeakers throughout the hall.

"A point of order, Brother President," he said.

"What is your point of order?" the president inquired casually.

"My point of order is that we have a constitutional amendment coming up tonight to discontinue saluting the flag as a protest against our country's foreign policy. Tonight is the third reading. It must be voted on tonight, as per the constitution, and I heard no mention of it in the agenda. When and where do you plan to take up this matter, Brother President?"

"Our first order of business," the president replied, "is to take up old business, of which there are several items. Our second order of business is to take up new business. I have decided to place the constitutional amendment dealing the pledge of allegiance after old business and before new business . . ."

"I have a motion, Brother President," the man at the mike said, interrupting.

"A motion is not in order at this time," the president responded. "We haven't even read the minutes of the previous meeting yet."

"I beg to differ, Brother President. You yourself introduced the reading of the agenda. So a motion on the agenda is in order, unless you are ruling yourself out of order."

The president thought in silence for a few moments. A number of the rank and file had risen from their seats and were making their way outside again. Others started to join them. A small exodus appeared to be taking place. I had seen Harry Bridges before the meeting began, down by the podium talking to rank-and-filers, but now he was nowhere to be seen. Eric Hoffer was seated all by himself, almost in the middle of the center section, looking over a handful of leaflets he had collected from various people who were passing them out to whomever would accept them outside the union hall earlier. Only longshoremen were permitted inside the hall during the meeting.

"What is your motion?" the president said, finally.

"My motion is that we move the constitutional amendment up to the first order of business under old business. Do I hear a second?" he demanded, looking around him with confidence. The men behind him standing in line to speak and the men at the other two microphones gave him a hearty "second." There was a scattering of very loud "NOs!" from the assemblage. The hall was now about half empty.

"I have no objection to that motion," the president stated. "The motion is now open for debate. There appear to be a number of speakers, so I am limiting debate to three minutes per speaker. Starting over here with the maker of the motion, the first speaker is Brother Brown. Brother Brown?"

Brother Brown turned and faced the gathered longshoremen still remaining in the hall. He made a brief impassioned speech condemning American foreign policy as a war-mongering threat to world peace and called upon the assembled longshoremen to proclaim publicly their opposition to what was essentially a fascist police state by publicly refusing, from this time forward, to pledge allegiance to it. He then sat down and the president nodded toward the man first in line at the center microphone. The man at the center microphone gave essentially the same speech, urged passage of the new amendment, and added that the secretary be instructed to send letters to all the local newspapers informing them of this longshore action. About halfway through a similar speech by the third speaker I decided to go outside myself and see what was happening. Since the hall was now about half empty, outside must be where all the action was.

Out in the parking lot longshoremen were scattered about in small groups. Car trunks were up and whiskey in plastic glasses was being passed around openly. Laughter and talk was taking place everywhere. I saw Harry Bridges, briefly, in the flare of a lighted match touched to a cigarette. He was standing in a group tipping his head back, taking a swig from someone's bottle. I wandered around until I ran into someone I knew, a new man like me, with whom I had worked that afternoon. We talked for a while, and then we noticed that there appeared to be a general drift of men back into the meeting, so we joined them.

Seated in the balcony of the hall once again I discovered that there was only one speaker left, at the center floor microphone. He was joined shortly by a tall, thin, graying man, who appeared somewhat agitated. As the latest speaker finished, the president looked at the ceiling, then at his watch, and then spoke.

"I'm inclined to cut off debate at this point," he said. "But so far all we have heard from are speakers for this amendment. Are there any speakers against it who wish to be heard?" The tall, thin, graying man raised his hand. "Yes, Brother Asher. You have the floor," said the president.

"Fellas," Brother Asher said, taking the mike in his hand and turning to face his audience, "I urge you to vote this amendment down. I'm against American foreign policy, too. But this amendment isn't going to do a damn thing to influence American foreign policy. All its gonna do is make us look like assholes. I urge you to vote it down. Imagine. Everybody's going to say we're anti-American." He surrendered the microphone to another man, short and balding, who had joined him in line.

"Yeah, Shorty. You got the floor," the president said, glancing at his watch again.

"What's the motion?" Shorty asked.

"Read the motion," the president said, turning to the secretary. The secretary read the motion.

"I have an amendment," said Shorty.

"What is your amendment?" said the president.

"This is a very serious matter," Shorty said. "I move that we put it on the ballot next fall when we elect our new officers and then the whole membership can vote on it."

Brother Brown jumped up and grabbed the mike out of Shorty's hand. "He can't do that," Brown screamed at the president.

"Why not?"

"Because . . ." Brother Brown sputtered. "Because . . . because the amendment is not germane to the motion, er, to the amendment to the constitution . . . that is."

"Are you telling me that an amendment concerning voting procedure is not germane to the motion being voted on?" the president asked.

"Uh . . . yes," said Brown.

"Well, I'm ruling that Shorty's amendment is properly before the membership. If you don't like it," the president said deliberately to Brother Brown, "then vote against it." He turned back to the audience as a whole.

"Men, we have quite a lot of business to get through tonight so we're . . ."

"I challenge the chair!" shouted Brother Brown.

If the president were irritated he did not show it. His speech, which had appeared almost bored at times, now became a monotone, as if he were reading from text. "The chair has been challenged. The constitution calls upon the vice-president to assume the chair in this situation. The vice-president, however, is in Los Angeles at a coast safety committee meeting. In the absence of the vice-president, the secretary will preside." The secretary finished a sentence he was writing, rose, and the president handed him the gavel.

"The chair has been challenged," the secretary said. "The procedure is as follows: The challenger and the president will each have five minutes to present their case. There will be no other speakers. The challenger will speak first. At the conclusion of the president's defense, the membership will vote either to support the challenger, or to sustain the chair. Brother Brown, you have the floor."

Brother Brown vehemently defended the sanctity of the union constitution, which described precisely how amendments were to be added. There were to be three readings of the proposed amendment at three successive union meetings. At the end of the third reading, the amendment was to be voted on. The constitution authorized no other procedures. No man is above the constitution, he said, not even the president. Brother Brown urged every member present to support him by supporting the constitution and his challenge to the chair.

The president defended his action to accept the amendment to postpone the vote and put it on the ballot at the next election by the fact that there appeared to be less than twenty percent of the membership present to vote, that the entire membership should shoulder the responsibility in making a decision of such magnitude as the one before us at this time, and, of course the vote would then be by secret ballot. He also stated rhetorically that no one is above the constitution, of course, but that the president, in matters of dispute, was the interpreter of the constitution. He then sat down.

The secretary conducted the vote, which was by a raise of hands.

The sergeant-at-arms counted the vote. The chair was sustained by approximately ten to one. The secretary turned the gavel back over to the president.

"Men, thank you for supporting the chair. We will now vote on the motion itself—to put the issue on the ballot next fall. But before we do, I want to tell you that we have quite a lot of business to get through tonight. There is some trouble in the East Bay, there is a motion coming out of the executive board to promote more men to the winch-board, and our International president, Harry Bridges, wants to say a few words." He looked around him. "Where the hell is Harry?" he asked the secretary. The secretary shrugged and shook his head. The president turned back to the assembly. "Well, anyway," he said, "do I hear a motion to close debate on the amendment to put this issue on the ballot next fall?"

Brother Brown and his followers objected to closing debate. The president put it to a vote of the membership. The membership voted overwhelmingly to close debate. The president then put the amendment itself, finally, to a vote.

"We will vote on the amendment to the amendment first," he said. "If the amendment to the amendment passes, it carries the amendment and the motion and the issue of whether we continue to pledge allegiance, or not, will be on the ballot next fall. All in favor for the amendment to the amendment raise your hands. The sergeant-at-arms and those helping him will do the counting." As a new man the only comment I could think of was "whew!" What a lot procedural machinery to go through to get something done. However, I had to admire the fact that the union was functioning, however slowly.

The amendment to the amendment carried overwhelmingly, with only Brother Brown, his colleagues, and a few others scattered about the hall voting against it. The following fall the original amendment calling for an end to the pledge of allegiance was defeated by a vote of approximately ten to one. As one old-timer put it to me then: "Hell, I don't like standing up and saluting the flag either. What am I, back in the fifth grade? But I had to support it. What the hell?"

The trouble in the East Bay had to do with someone other than longshoremen working cargo at a long unused pier on the Oakland estuary. No vessel was tied up at the pier as of yet, but someone had hired temporary labor on a daily basis to assemble the cargo on pallet boards for eventual shipment by vessel to the Far East. The officers were bringing the matter before the membership to seek approval of a course of action consisting of several steps. First, set up a picket line in front of the pier to stop all incoming truck cargo. Second, pursue some form of legal action if any one member of the employer group was in violation of the labor contract. And third, inform the steamship companies that any vessel attempting to load that cargo would not be worked, and, furthermore, notify the other ports up and down the coast of our action and request a boycott of said vessel if it showed up in their area.

The first response to the officer's recommendation was from an angry rank-and-filer who seized one of the floor microphones. "Longshore work is longshore work," he stated. "I move we collect some guys tomorrow morning, go over to that pier, and break some goddamn legs." He received a hearty cheer, but after discussion the officer's recommendation was agreed on by general acclamation in lieu of a formal vote.

The question of whether to promote more men to the winch-driver's board from the hold-board was a complicated issue and drew heated response from people on both sides of the question. In the port of San Francisco longshoremen are historically dispatched to jobs from one of five boards. The hold-board means working general cargo aboard ship, either on deck or down in the hold. The dock-board handles general cargo on the dock, sorting the cargo, stacking it on pallet-boards, etc. There jobs are for men, usually older men, who prefer not to work aboard ship anymore; their reasons may be that they do not like to rig ship's gear, climb up and down ladders, or whatever. The forklift, winch, and crane boards are so-called skilled jobs, and seniority is the criteria for getting on one of these boards. If on any given day there are more winch or lift jobs than there are certified men available to cover these jobs, the chief dispatcher will announce to the hold-board that holdmen can, on a one-day basis, volunteer to drive winches, forklifts, or cranes. This always precipitates a scramble on the part of holdmen to pick up one of those jobs and get a vacation from working coffee, cotton, drums, or discharging bananas for the day. On the other hand, if, as occasionally happens, there are not enough winch or lift jobs to clean those boards, the winch and forklift drivers can volunteer for surplus jobs off the hold-board, and work coffee, drums, cotton, or bananas for that one day. That is, pick up and move weight the old-fashioned way by using their backs instead of raising and lowering levers to accomplish the task. When this situation occurs one rarely witnesses a mad stampede toward the hold-board dispatch window on the part of the winch, lift, and crane drivers.

The fifth board off which men are dispatched is the dock-exemption board, sometimes called the sick, lame, or lazy board, where men who have been injured can find temporary light work—even permanent light work, in some cases—until they recover sufficiently to participate in the regular longshore work routine once again.

The recommendation to promote men to the winch-board came

from the Executive Board, which consists of thirty-five men elected annually along with all the other officers in the union. The Executive Board is the policy-making board of the union. All recommendations from that body are brought to the rank and file for approval. Most of their recommendations are routinely passed by voice vote without debate, but any motion having to do with how the work is done or who does it is destined to receive detailed attention and heated discussion. The precise wording of the motion read: "To promote a total of sixty men from the hold-board to the winch-board, forty to winches on days and twenty to night-winches." Fork-lift drivers were not mentioned, but to them the motion was ominous: they were next. Men were lined up at all three microphones before the president had finished reading the motion.

The first man to speak was an old winch-driver called "Crank," and he was against the motion. "The Exec-Board is trying to flood our board," he said. "I only got out on four jobs last week. The Exec-Board has been taken over by the holdmen. They all vote for each other. Now they're trying to promote themselves to the winches. None of us will make a living." He sat down amid hoots and hollers. "That's it, crank it up another notch, Crank," someone shouted. Crank had a reputation among holdmen of bringing another load of cargo into the hold from the dock before the holdmen had finished stowing the one before.

The next speaker was for the motion. His name was Mortonson and he pointed out that if proof was needed to add men to the winch-board it lay in the fact that, even with all the deaths and retirements, no one had been added to the skilled boards in over three years. It was only fair that the motion be passed. The next speaker sandbagged Mortonson.

"Mort," he said without introducing himself, "isn't it true that if this motion passes you will be among the first to be promoted? And aren't you a member of the Executive Board?" The statement brought on waves of hoots, hollers, and laughter. It also brought Mort, red faced and angry, back to the microphone.

"You've already spoken," the president said to Mort when he had finally rapped the membership back to order. "You've had your turn at the mike."

"My reputation and integrity have been attacked," Mort shouted. "I demand a chance to respond."

"Okay, but make it short," the president said. "It's getting late and I'm clocking everybody."

"Yeah," Mort said fiercely, turning to face his audience. "Yeah, I'm a member of the Executive Board, and yeah, I'm going to be promoted. But, so what? Just listen to this: In the last three years over fifty men have retired from Local 10, and almost all of them were off the skill boards. And Crank? Crank got only four days last week? Hell, I got four days myself on the winches by volunteering off the hold-board. And one of them was Sunday, an overtime day. If Crank didn't get more than four days, it's because he flopped!" A man flops when his number is called and he does not answer the call to pick up the job. By the Local 10 dispatch rules a man who flops has to take twenty-four hours off work. The president asked Crank if he wanted to answer Mort. Crank remained seated.

Several speakers spoke heatedly on both sides of the question, and then Shorty appeared at a microphone again, apparently from nowhere. "What's before us?" he asked. The president had the secretary read the motion. "I have an amendment," Shorty said again.

"What's your amendment?"

"My amendment is that we add half the number the motion calls for to the winch-board now, and add the other half to the board as the men retire and create vacancies."

Shorty's amendment was seconded from various places throughout the hall. Immediately another man stepped up to the microphone and called for the question.

"The question has been called for," the president said. "All those in favor of cutting off debate say 'Aye.' " A roar of "Ayes" came from the crowded hall. "Okay, all those opposed?" A roar, but a smaller roar, of "Nos" filled the hall.

"The motion to cut off debate has carried," the president said. "We will now vote on the main motion. We will vote first on Shorty's amendment. If Shorty's amendment carries, it carries both the amendment and the main motion. All in favor of the amendment say 'Aye.' " I decided that, whoever was president, it would be sort of handy to have someone like Shorty around and maybe a few others with his talents.

There was a roar of "Ayes" and there was an almost equal roar of "Nos." The president declared himself in doubt as to the outcome and repeated the vote by having everyone stand in turn to support his position. The motion carried by a yes vote of about sixty percent.

Harry Bridges, a slight, thin man of medium height weighing no more than perhaps one hundred and fifty pounds, certainly was not the type the public thinks of as the typical beefy longshoreman. He had immigrated to America from Australia when a very young man and still retained traces of an Aussie accent. Starting when he first came to prominence during the strikes in the middle thirties, he had been under attack by both the ship owners and the federal government, which had tried for almost twenty years to deport him back to his original homeland. The Department of Justice's charge against him—through the Bureau of Immigration—was that he had lied on his application to become a citizen: they said he was a member of the Communist Party, and he had said he was not. No concrete connection, like a membership card, had ever been produced by the Department of Justice, so Harry retained his citizenship and remained in America. He also rose to and remained president of the entire International Longshore and Warehouse Union, on the West Coast, Hawaii, and wherever else they existed.

The attitude of the rank-and-file members to their International president ranged from outright adulation through political cynicism to, in a few cases, bitter hatred. But when it got down to the nitty-gritty they all backed him to a man, to a woman, us against *them*. At one time in the late forties the federal government, through the Department of Labor and with the help of the Congress of Industrial Organizations, had held a plebiscite among ILWU members that entirely backfired on them. The Congress of Industrial Organizations had thrown the ILWU out of its congress. The scenario called for the CIO to come back in by holding a jurisdictional election. The ballot was simple: Do you want a new union under the auspices of the CIO, or do you wish to remain with the ILWU? Yes or No?

The Department of Labor set up and manned voting booths in all the longshore locals up and down the West Coast and waited for the longshoremen to cast their ballots. It was not the results of the count that so startled the authorities, but the outcome of their efforts. The ILWU leadership put out the word to boycott the proceedings and nobody voted. From San Diego to Seattle not a single ballot was cast, one way or another. After that, the federal government backed off on their efforts to destroy Harry Bridges and the ILWU, and the ship owners began to seek an accommodation with West Coast longshoremen. The us-against-them mentality still remained, however, not only with Harry Bridges, but with large numbers of the rank and file: There may be individuals within the government and the judiciary who were decent people, but those organizations themselves were out to get the American working stiff, and you were better off having nothing to do with them.

"We 'ave some new members 'ere tonight," Harry Bridges started out his talk, "and aye say, 'Welcome!' But I want to tell you new guys. We 'ave some scissor-bills among us. Don't listen to them. They just want to rip everything up. Keep yer eyes open and yer nose clean and you'll be all right. Just remember what aye said." International President Bridges then went on to caution the membership and make them aware of the various evils the anti-labor forces in America hoped to impose on the working guy and that the only defense against these wealthy bosses, who owned the courts and the government and the newspapers, was eternal vigilance and working-class unity. He then remarked on a variety of other subjects of both national and international import. He ended up castigating the American government for setting off enormous underground nuclear explosions in southern Nevada, which, he could personally attest, made the earth tremble all the way to Las Vegas. When Bridges turned to give the microphone back to the president, a member seized one of the floor mikes down in front.

"Harry!" he yelled. "What do you think of this amendment?"

"What amendment?" Bridges asked, bending into the microphone once again.

"The one about saluting the flag," the man shouted.

"Saluting the flag?" Bridges asked, puzzled. Apparently he had been outside during the entire hassle. "Saluting the flag? Wot the 'ell's that got to do with me? Why do you need an amendment? If you don't want to salute the flag, don't salute it. Wot the 'ell." He turned and left the stage.

Another man grabbed a floor mike. "I move we adjourn," he said.

"No," someone shouted. "We can't adjourn. We got to . . ."

"A motion to adjourn is always in order," the president of the local interrupted him. "All those in favor of adjournment say 'Aye.' "

Amid the roar of "Ayes" everyone raced to the dispatch windows to get their books stamped proving they had attended the meeting.

It had been an interesting meeting. Harry Bridges had come out against underground testing of nuclear bombs in Nevada, but he had failed to mention that the Russians had been exploding the same in the atmosphere over the USSR, or that the French were also preparing to do so on an island near Tahiti in the South Pacific.

I had been watching Eric Hoffer down on the lower floor of the auditorium. For the last half of the meeting he had been taking notes, it appeared, especially during Bridges' speech. His notes were on a piece of paper, which he had abandoned along with the small pile of leaflets on the seat next to him when he rushed off to get his book stamped. I made my way downstairs through the crowd to where he had been seated and picked up the papers. Eric Hoffer had been doing a crossword puzzle.

I never did find out what the old business on the agenda was for that night.

Chapter Four

Cargo

When I came on the waterfront all cargo aboard ship was stowed and discharged by hand and every longshoreman carried a hook and a pair of heavy work gloves. It was always useful to have a variety of hooks available to work with. We found that the large cargo hooks, the ones you saw Marlon Brando's colleagues using in *On The Waterfront,* were only useful working cotton. Then a hook that size came in handy. With its long handle sticking out on both sides of the shaft, you could swing it down, bite into the bale, and then plant your feet and lift with your whole body. Sometimes you had to lift cotton instead of rolling it; there is no other way to move a bale a couple of inches or so if you have to take up some slack. But if you were not working cotton, a big hook was a nuisance to have around. There is no way to carry it except in your hand. It will not fit into your hip pocket, like a smaller hook, and who the hell wants to shove it under his belt and go off to lunch with the handle poking him in the stomach?

In that movie all the longshoremen carried their hooks, big hooks, with the point down hanging from their shoulders whether they were working cargo or not. They probably slept with the damn things. I never saw anyone carry his hook the way they did in the movie, and I cannot imagine how anyone could do it. If it is to remain in place and not fall off with every movement you make, it has to hook into something. If it is your shoulder it is hooking into, it hurts. Once, while working in Los Angeles, I drew a longshoreman from New York as a partner. I asked him about it: Do New York longshoremen really pack their hooks around that way?

"I never did," he replied. "Nobody else I knew did either."

He had seen the movie, too, and we conjectured about the film. Most of the longshoremen portrayed in it were ridiculous, we agreed, as were their work practices, so the way they carried their hooks could have simply been dreamed up by whoever made the movie. A barely possible explanation had been offered by an older longshoreman with whom the New Yorker had been working at the time the movie came out. Many years before, the old-timer had recalled, longshoremen could not carry their hooks in their hip pocket. If they got into a fight, the cops would arrest them for carrying a concealed weapon. That, we agreed, was ridiculous. Neither the New Yorker nor I could ever recall seeing hooks being used in a fight. It looks like a wicked weapon, but it would be awkward to wield. Also, if you did use it, swung a hook at someone, and missed, the guy you were fighting with might feel free to use something even more lethal on you. The only time I ever heard of a longshoreman using a hook on someone was in a dispute with a walking boss that took place years before I came on the waterfront. The walking boss was down in the bottom of the hold, and he and the longshoreman got into an argument over how the gang was going to stow the cargo. The argument became heated, whereupon the walking boss told the man he was fired. When the walking boss turned and started to climb the ladder out of the hatch, the longshoreman buried his hook in the walking boss's ass. It was a gross act, but apparently not irresolvable. They were both still working on the waterfront when I came on the scene.

I owned a variety of hooks. In addition to a big cotton hook, I used a smaller general cargo hook, a sack-hook with five curved-in tines, which was absolutely essential when working coffee, and a Japanese hook. The Japanese hook was everybody's favorite. It was simply a light wooden shaft about a foot or so long with a small hook on one end and a small knob on the other end that fit neatly into the palm of your hand. It was very practical. It gave you an extra-long reach and you could use it on just about everything. Whenever we opened the hatch on a Japanese ship there was a scramble to get down below first and see if the Japanese longshoremen had left any of their hooks behind. We had to buy our hooks, but the Japanese longshoremen must have been issued them on a daily basis because they left a lot of them aboard ship. It was very generous of them, and we appreciated their gifts. If you found a Japanese hook when you opened up the hatch, it just about made your day no matter how hard you had to work discharging their cargo. I still have all my old hooks, but it is the Japanese hooks I really treasure.

Gloves—work gloves that is—have changed with automation. There is still a lot of heavy, greasy equipment and wire cables to haul around by hand, both on the dock and aboard ship, but much of longshore work now is driving equipment. If you are driving a crane, a forklift, a straddle-truck, or a semitractor, big cumbersome gloves just get in your way. When driving equipment, light, supple, soft leather gloves are the preferred item of wear—not Jack and Jennys.

All work gloves used to be made out of muleskin. I do not know if it was tougher leather than horsehide or not, but the top-quality, heavy work glove was purported to be muleskin. The proof of it was on the glove itself. On the back of your right-hand glove was stamped the profile head of a mule. Below it was the legend "Jack." On your left-hand glove there was a picture of "Jenny." Actually, there were two brands of muleskin gloves that were in competition with each other. The other brand was called "Maude and Claude." The mules may have looked a little different, but except for their brand name, the gloves were identical.

The rest of the classic longshore uniform was made up of black jeans, a hickory shirt, and a white cloth cap. The cap was the first to go when wearing hard hats became mandatory. Hickory shirts are still around, but fewer and fewer stores stock them, so they are sometimes hard to find. Stevedores simply stopped wearing them, especially the younger, black longshoremen. I liked the shirts because they were tough, meaning they did not rip easily, and they were long sleeved and had two breast pockets. As time went on and they went through wash after wash, they got softer and softer. If you bought your work clothes in the fall of the year, by the following summer they had lost a lot of their weight and were just right for working in warm weather.

One brand of hickory shirts was called Big Ben and had a picture of a gorilla embroidered into the fabric just above the left breast pocket. As a work shirt it was supposed to be as tough as a gorilla. We occasionally worked the Alameda Navy Base, and when we worked there we had to show a pass with our picture on it to get past the gate. Among our longshore brothers was a big black man named J. J., who was known as the ugliest man in the world. When I wore my Big Ben shirt the younger black guys used to point to the gorilla and say, "Hey? How come you're wearing J. J's Navy pass?"

The cargo we worked came in all shapes and sizes and, literally, from all the countries of the world. I once discharged helicopter blades, being sent back from Japan for realignment, that were stowed on top of bales of horsehair from Outer Mongolia. I worked that horsehair only once, but it was memorable for being absolutely and totally infested with fleas, very hungry fleas after their long voyage from the Orient. The worst discharge cargo to work had to be bones. Dry cattle bones came in from the Argentine which we shoveled into hampers that were dumped into railroad gondola cars on the dock and shipped to I don't know where. The bones were dry, very dry, and although they did not make a very heavy shovelful, they raised considerable clouds of dust when you heaved them into the hamper. Nothing you could tie around your face could keep that bone dust out of your nose and eyes.

Since all longshore jobs are dispatched in sequence according to the hours worked, having low hours means one has first pick of the jobs in the morning. One did not choose bones, of course. They were left to the very end of the dispatch for the hungry men who tried to work every day of the year. But there was other cargo to be avoided, also. Raw steer hides, which I have described in another book, with a scoop of manure heaped into the folded skin (the maggots ate the manure and not the hide) were nasty. We loaded them out to Korea and Japan as raw, slimy skins, and they came back as baseball mitts and shoe leather. We handled them twice, the second time with a great deal more enthusiasm than the first.

Automation in the form of seagoing vans first began to appear on the waterfront in the late sixties. The first vans were small, some only the size of a big closet. They gradually grew larger until the twenty-foot metal container became standard, although by the mid-seventies the vast majority of vans were forty foot or longer. When the larger containers came into use and were sent across the Pacific, not all of them came back. Finally the shipping companies sent agents over there to chase them down and find out what had happened to them. They found that a lot of them in Southeast Asia had been barged up the rivers and remained there, as homes. Whole families were living in them. They were wonderful shelter from the rain, it was not very hard to cut windows into them, and if raised up and placed on stanchions at the four corners, they were relatively bug-free and of course not subject to termite damage.

The vans as cargo containers came onto the waterfront gradually, but their use was fostered in every way, even by the U.S. government. A container, since it was locked onto the ship, was deemed legally to be part of the vessel. It was additionally decreed that after it was discharged it remained a segment of the ship until the seal was broken and the doors were opened. This gave the van a lot of slack. After it was transported inland, perhaps thousands of miles, it still remained maritime. Places like Oklahoma City became ports. A good portion of the containers had goods in them consigned to several different receivers, all in the same van. These were called LCLs, less than carload lots. These vans had to be opened and their cargo sorted and consolidated and then reshipped so that every receiver got the right freight. This was to be our longshore work, to make up for the jobs we had lost through automation. However, Oklahoma City and several other cities in mostly southern states with anti-union laws on their books offered labor at one-third of West Coast longshore wages. Eventually, this work bypassed us entirely.

Among the first cargo to be placed in vans were raw hides. I don't think many longshoremen regretted their absence from our work scene. But as time went on and more and more cargo went into vans we watched a good portion of our work disappear. We still had steel I-beams and long pipe to work, and automobiles and other cargo that did not lend itself to being stowed in containers. On a tonnage basis, however, both the import and export of containers became the bulk of the cargo we worked. Ships and the way they were loaded, waterfront practices that had existed almost unchanged for hundreds of years, disappeared completely in a little over a decade. The waterfront would never be the same again. Our problem became how to deal with it. The shipping interests were clamoring to cut our manning scale to the bone through a program they called "Mechanization and Modernization." Negotiations dragged on. Finally the employer group and our International Union leadership came up with an agreement in the early seventies. It was immediately rejected by rank-and-file longshoremen up and down the West Coast.

The contract consisted essentially of an agreement to cut the gang size from eight holdmen to four in return for management's guarantee to pay the equivalent of thirty-six hours wages to those thrown out of work and sitting at home. The shipping interest's intent was to reduce the work force by attrition; those who retired or died would not be replaced.

"They're trying to buy our jobs, and our jobs aren't for sale," was the longshore cry. They meant the next generation's jobs, of course, those of their sons, and later, daughters.

Through a diligent campaign on the part of both management and the union officials, in addition to a substantial pay raise and a provision for early retirement, opposition to the proposed contract was worn down until it finally passed on a coastwide secret ballot, barely. The opposition's cry that it was a buyout turned out to be correct. Over the next dozen years the number of longshoremen in San Francisco dropped from five thousand to less than fifteen hundred. Furthermore, almost half of the remaining fifteen hundred were unemployed, sitting at home drawing the pay guarantee because there was not enough work to go around. To make matters even worse, those men still on the job were working harder than ever since the cargo not placed in vans—and there was still a lot of it—was being worked with half as many men as before, with one man doing the work of two.

In many ways the men working cargo understood the problem much better than their leadership, and initiated their own solutions. Devices to speed up the movement of freight over the waterfront were nothing new; historically they had been in place all along. Two hundred years ago cargo was hoisted by men heaving on a rope. Then they invented the steam-winch to lift cargo. When the first forklift was brought into the hold to stow prepalletized cargo aboard ship (actually two forklifts, one offshore and one inshore), the gang got together and, after a brief conference, flipped a coin to see who got to drive first and who got to sit down. Production increased tremendously and the longshoremen took their share of what was gained by taking it easier on the job, essentially shortening their workday.

Seeing a worker sitting down is absolutely intolerable and unacceptable to management—when he or she is on the payroll, that is. Seeing the unemployed sitting down, however, arouses no response among management whatsoever, even if they created those unemployed. Consequently, eliminating work was not the primary aim of the employer's Mechanization and Modernization program. Eliminating workers was. It was at about this time and in response to all this that I became politically active in the union and began to run for union office.

I was first elected to the Exccutive Board, and then much later to the office of vice-president. I was also elected as a representative from San Francisco to the All Coast Longshore Caucus. While holding these offices I continued to work full time on the waterfront. Except for the president, the secretary, and the business agents, nobody makes a living off the union. And even those full-time officeholders have to go back to work again after two years in their posts. It is a way of keeping the officers close to the men and the work, and it is unquestionably successful. There is nothing like the reality of work to instruct you in what is important to those doing it. If you are going to hold office in any of the longshore locals on the West Coast and perform your duties successfully, the smartest thing you can do is listen to the men you work with. The best analysis of the Mechanization and Modernization contract I ever heard was delivered by a longshoreman one morning while the both of us were standing in line waiting to get a job.

Linc—short for Lincoln—was a black man a bit older than me who was born in the South, worked around here and there, and eventually found his way to the San Francisco waterfront. He and I got jobs together occasionally when our work hours coincided.

"You know," Linc said, "the companies fought us tooth and nail to stop us from working on and off. Now they have set up a situation where half the men are working, and the other half are home, sitting on their ass. The companies have set up their own on-and-off. You can bet your life we are going to pay for it. I'd rather have the guys back on the job."

How deeply and how severely we were going to pay for it, and in how many unknown ways, eventually became evident. A few years after that conversation with Linc, I was elected vice-president, and about a month into my term, I became party to a decision to shut down work on a ship. A stevedore company decided, unilaterally, to do away with two jobs. Actually, they weren't doing away with them; they were equipment jobs and they were going to have someone other than longshoremen perform that work. We had got to the point where the loss of any more work was unacceptable, and two jobs were two jobs. It was a clear violation of the contract, but the company was adamant. They were going to do it and to hell with us. We officers conferred, and we decided we had no choice. We shut down the ship. The following week all the idle men in the Port of San Francisco were denied their pay guarantee, a form of dole given to those for whom there was no work. The companies were holding the men's money hostage until we gave in. At a union meeting the men backed us one hundred percent, so we hung tough and we did not work the ship. The following week the men were denied pay guarantee again. This gave us all pause, made us check our hole card. If you are a union official it is hard to persist in a questionable course that will deny seven or eight hundred longshoremen their paycheck Friday. One other officer and I wanted to hang tough and shut down the whole port. If they were going to up the ante, we could too, and make it so expensive they would fold. If we backed down now, it would open a floodgate, and next time the employers would want even more. We were outvoted. So we lost two more jobs.

I wonder how many Jack and Jennys they are selling in Oklahoma City.

CHAPTER FIVE

Timber!

I know of no blue-collar industry whose work forces have not been seriously depleted by new technology and automation. All industries have been hit in their own unique way. The lumber industry provides an example all its own.

Trees in the forest used to be cut down by hand using saws and axes. Frequently it would take several men all day to fall and trim one sizable spruce or fir and cut it up into manageable lengths to be dragged down a logging road to a river where rafts were made up to be floated downstream to the mill. Now, using power saws, trees are felled, trimmed, and cut to size in a fraction of that time, and lifted out to some assembly point by hot air balloons or helicopters. You don't hear much chop, chop, chop in the woods anymore. Now its an ear shattering whine as some piece of equipment revs itself up to provide us with two-by-fours.

One of my father's first jobs, he once told me, was working in the woods for a tree-faller. The tree-faller, the man who actually decided where the cuts were to be made to fall the tree in the desired direction, was, along with the tree-topper, considered to be the top lumberjack in the forest. The faller was generally conceded, then and now, to possess the most skill. The topper merely had to be crazy.

The topper, with a small axe dangling from a line attached to his belt, climbed the tree until he got up to where the diameter of the trunk was reduced to about a foot— anything less than that was considered useless for lumber—and chopped the top off there. The moment of truth came with the last blow of his axe when the remaining length of the tree above him began to lean over and then break away from the lower trunk. In first-growth timber, the topper was frequently 150 or more feet above the ground, and even though he was secured to the trunk below the cut by a heavy leather belt and his spiked feet were dug in, he was whipped savagely back and forth when the top portion fell away. He had, literally, to hang on for dear life. Sometimes a falling limb would smack him as the top dropped away, knocking his grip loose. Then, perhaps half conscious, he would fall until he could dig his spikes in again or until the leather belt, sliding down the other side of the trunk, caught on something and jerked him to a stop. As he climbed the tree the topper had to hack off and clear away occasional branches, especially near the top where he had to make room to swing his axe and make his cut. It was dangerous, it was hard work, and all of it was done so that when the tree was finally felled it did not catch on other trees and perhaps destroy them or itself on the way down.

The topper worked alone at a lonely job. The faller, however, rated a helper. My father, when a teenager, was a faller's helper.

"Did they yell 'TIMBER!' " I asked, "when the tree started to fall?" I was just a kid.

"Huh?" my father replied.

"You know, like in the movies?" I said.

"Hell, no. Nobody had to be told to get out of the way."

A tree randomly cut down can fall in any direction. But if the falling tree is not carefully placed it might, in addition to taking other trees with it, even shatter its own trunk if it does not land on a bed of boughs laid out to receive it and cushion its fall. Also the faller has to place the tree where it can be worked, the remaining limbs trimmed off, and the trunk cut up into the desired lengths. A faller who does this with accuracy is still a valuable man in the woods, and his prestige is usually tops among his fellow workers.

In the old days trees were felled using a combination of axes and long-toothed, wide-bladed, flexible saws six to eight feet in length or even longer with men on each end pulling against each other. The lumber company furnished the saws, but the lumberjack, the faller, carried his own axes, and no one else was allowed to touch them. There were usually two axes, sometimes three. They were double edged. When not being used the heads were wrapped in heavy, oiled felt and then encased in leather to keep them rust-free and keen. Every night the faller honed their edges down in preparation for to-morrow's attack on more trees.

The faller's boy was his all-around assistant—my father must have been around fifteen or sixteen at the time—almost his servant. When moving around from camp to camp the faller carried his axes while the faller's boy carried everything else. In my father's case it was a big steamer trunk, heavy as hell, as he described it, which he lugged from train depot to a buggy or a Model T Ford, and finally to the faller's own personal tent when they got to the new camp. The faller never opened the trunk in my father's presence, so only once did he get to see what was inside it that made it so heavy.

My father's job was to work wherever he was needed, but his duty to his faller came first. Trees were cut down sometimes fifteen feet above ground level, up where the clear grain of the trunk was well started, away from the swollen bole near the earth. The faller got to that height by creating a series of steps out of shakes and shingles about a foot apart that he drove into small precise cuts he made in the trunk of the tree. Taking a chop up, and then a chop down, the faller, cutting cleanly through the bark to the clear grain of the wood, would remove and then enlarge a small wedge cut out of the tree. My father hauled the shakes and shingles up the tree behind him and stood ready. When the faller was satisfied with his cut he turned and selected a shake from a fanlike array my father held out to him, standing on the step below. He drove the shake into the cut at right angles to the tree with the flat of the axe blade. Then he took a shingle, which is much thinner than a shake, placed it into the cut beneath the shake and hammered it in, tightening up the shake even more. That step being done, he advanced up, stood on the shake, and tested it with his weight. Then he began making another cut. They progressed that way, the faller and my father, working their way up and around the trunk of the tree, the faller cutting his precise little notches followed by my father with an armload of shakes and shingles. When they got to where the faller wanted the sawyers to begin their cut, he marked it out clearly in the bark with his axe. The sawyers also did their work standing on shakes protruding from the trunk of the tree, sawing back and forth sometimes twenty feet above the ground. But the sawyers made their own little platforms, not the faller. After all, they were the ones who had to stand on them.

After the faller had seen to it that the sawyers were started correctly, he and my father went around to the other side of the tree and constructed another set of steps up to where the faller would make his undercut, which would take place when the sawyers had cut about halfway through the other side of the tree.

There was excitement born of turmoil in the West in those days. The last of the frontier and the Indian wars were only a generation or so behind those men now working in the mines and the forests. Labor militancy, born in the mines of the Rocky Mountains, had spread west through the lumber camps and finally to the coast to team up with an old-world brand of radicalism nourished by the European immigrants among the longshoremen and seamen. Militant tracts and leaflets calling for action were everywhere, and labor disputes were a constant fact of a worker's life. The mine and mill owners fought their workers with all the political and police power on their side. State and private militias repeatedly broke up strikes with gunfire, and the police grabbed, beat up, and jailed every working-class leader who came to the fore. I once asked my father toward the end of his life what was the one thing that stood out most to him that the workers in the woods had won. He gave it only a moment's thought. "Sheets and blankets," he replied. "We got clean sheets and blankets every Sunday out there in the woods. A lumberjack didn't have to provide his own bedding anymore, traveling around with a bedroll on his back like a bindlestiff."

Since all work was temporary, men felt no loyalty to any one employer. They would quit one lumber company and move on to another whenever they felt the urge to do so. Sometimes it made no sense. One lumber camp looked pretty much the same as the next to my father, but his faller seemed to him to move on more often than anyone else. About every third week he would abruptly announce, "Kid, we're pulling up stakes tomorrow." Then my father would have to lug the big steamer trunk all over hell again.

Sunday was the lumberjack's day of rest, but it was really a day of recuperation from Saturday night when they would all go into the nearest town and raise hell. Everyone, that is, except for my father and another tree-faller's boy who were deemed too young to get drunk, get in fights, and make love to whores. They had to stay in camp.

"Keep an eye on my goods," the faller always told my father before he left, indicating the trunk. The trunk, as always, was secured shut with a big brass padlock. The faller's axes, lovingly wrapped and sheathed, were carefully placed on his cot with a blanket over them, put to bed, one could almost say. "And we'll be pulling out in the morning," he added this particular time.

With the camp deserted my father lay back on his cot, contemplating what to do. Almost immediately the other faller's kid stuck his head through the tent flap.

"Hey," he said, "there's a feller out here selling likker. You want some?"

"Hell, yes! What kind?"

My father and the other boy sat there in the tent drinking backwoods still liquor out of a gallon jug and exchanging the woes of being the lowest men on the totem pole in the lumber camp. My father was moving on again the next morning. His new friend expressed regret. By this time they were half drunk.

"And I have to carry that goddamn heavy trunk all over hell!"

What made it so heavy, his friend wanted to know? My father thought it over.

"Damned if I know," he said. "But I'm going to find out." He rose, went over to the faller's cot, threw back the blanket, and seized one of the axes.

The second blow of the axe sprung the lock, and my old man threw open the trunk. There was a clean change of work clothes on top. My father brushed them aside. Underneath, it was all paper.

Gathered on one side was a stack of leaflets urging the workers of the world to unite. Next to it another stack proclaimed "One Big Union." Another outlined the road to the triumph of syndicalism. The open trunk explained to my father why his tree-faller moved on from one lumber camp to another every three weeks. The man was a Wobbly organizer; a revolutionary monk dedicated to the triumph of the working class over their capitalist oppressors.

My father sat down to think over his discovery, but it took him only moments to make up his mind. He did not know which he was more frightened of: the tree-faller coming back and finding he had used one of the man's beloved axes to violate the privacy of his trunk, or some vigilante group of farmers coming in and finding him in possession of all this revolutionary literature. My father had gotten suddenly sober.

"Holy shit!" he exclaimed. He started throwing his few possessions together.

"What are you doing?" the other boy asked.

"I'm getting the hell out of here," my father replied.

"Wait for me," the other boy said, rushing out of the tent. "I'll get my stuff. I'm going with you."

The other boy's name turned out to be Bill Heine. They left that lumber camp without looking back. My father, however, must have absorbed something from that tree-faller, if not from his leaflets. He retained a soft spot in his heart for Wobbly principles for the rest of his life.

CHAPTER SIX

Through the Looking Glass

Economists are a curious and interesting people. Also they are very human. They try to stick to what they know, and, like the rest of us, they tend to avoid taking a position on actions that, although properly within their sphere of expertise, might lead to upsetting the status quo. For instance, if the Federal Reserve Board lowers the prime interest rate one-half of a percentage point, it will result in perhaps as many as 100,000 new housing starts in America. Economists can predict that and applaud the action in a stagnant economy because it will help get things moving again. Alternately, if the Fed raises the prime rate one-half of a percentage point—to combat an anticipated rise in inflation—it will possibly throw a quarter of a million carpenters, plumbers, electricians, and various other building trades people out of work. Economists are aware of this phenomenon, regret that it happens, but hesitate to recommend means to correct this social upheaval. The more forceful and confident of the economists among them will insist that those carpenters and others now unemployed must face reality and go get a job somewhere else. Where, McDonald's? Is that where economists go when they are out of work and looking for a job? Building trades workers have skills that should be used and not remain dormant, too.

If you want to make that forceful and confident economist uncomfortable, which admittedly is always tempting, you might ask him if housing starts shouldn't be based primarily upon the need for homes, rather than have shelter in America be dependent upon a manipulation of the prime interest rate? Since the need for housing is ongoing this might also stabilize the need for carpenters, plumbers, electricians, plus home appliances and the people who manufacture them. A word of caution here. If you bring up a subject like this with these people you are at risk of very quickly being banished from their midst. As they throw up their hands and back away from you, they will protest that a decision like that is political, outside their sphere of concern as economists. You might also get yourself called a Marxist, or, worse, a Communist, which will place you beyond the pale and unworthy of further discourse. You may reject Marxism and despise Communists, but labeling you one or the other is always an easy way of dismissing unwelcome questioners.

I have always found this a curious dismissal. Originally, all Marxists, starting with Karl, were economists. But that was a long time ago. Apparently time makes a difference in this discipline. Over the years I have met any number of Marxists, and Communists, and not more than one of them, possibly two, were truly economists. They were all political, of course, and stood foursquare for equality, justice, and democracy. As for the prime rate, their usual response was that it was manipulated by those holding power for their own interest. So what else is new? If pressed, a doctrinaire Marxist will further state that, in a Marxist society, money will be lent to those who need it. By a communist head of the Fed, of course. Well, why not? It worked so beautifully in Russia.

The best-paying blue-collar jobs in America are found in those industries that have the strongest trade unions. This is axiomatic, a given, analysts insist, and the statement is correlatively correct. It can be backed up by citing data from the U.S. Bureau of Labor Statistics. Whether it reflects reality or not is arguable. What about working conditions? If pressed for a response they will say that the answer is the same for both questions: good working conditions, just like wages, come from strong trade unions. What other answer could there possibly be? Here the economist's thinking gets a little fuzzy. And those hard-working people over at the Bureau of Labor Statistics who, for over six decades, have been trying to make sense of all this, are of no help. Actually, the Bureau of Labor Statistics has more to do with statistics than it has to do with labor. The second half of the economist's answer is simply false, and much of the first half is suspect, too.

Good working conditions on the job are created and secured by the people working the job. To go even further, I would insist that those clauses in union contracts dealing with working conditions were placed in those contracts after they had already been secured by the workers on the job. Those clauses merely codified a pre-existing condition. Frequently, what is put into print and guaranteed by the contract is considerably less than what the workers had already achieved before the contract was negotiated. The best example of this, because everybody has them, almost, are work breaks, relief periods on the job. A typical labor contract will specify a ten- or fifteen-minute break in the morning and the same in the afternoon. Prior to it having been written up, the workers invariably were covering each other on the job for their breaks and they were probably taking off whenever they felt the need, probably more than twice a day, and probably some of them for longer than fifteen minutes. Think of your own job and how you and the others work it out.

But now it is fifteen minutes and management gets to say when you can take your break because it is now written into the contract. Management, of course, is coming down hard to have the contract enforced.

Since the workers will insist in continuing to work in their same old way, not without some success, management will interpret their conduct as a violation of a sacred deal made between them and the union and will threaten dire consequences for this new infraction. They probably will not fire anyone offhand because that might affect production, so one of the first things they will do is get on the phone to the union. That is, call the business agent. I have actually seen B.A.s come down on the job in response to a call like this from the employer and tell the workers to obey the employer's commands. The first time I saw it happen I was in a group of six other workers, and at first none of us could believe our ears.

"What?" someone finally said. "What?"

"That's right," the business agent said, turning to the man. "The company is perfectly within their rights. It's right here in the contract in plain English. Fifteen minutes is all you get."

"Why, you dumb son of a bitch! Who do you think you're supposed to represent? You're trying to give away our working conditions!" We had to restrain the man. He was going to physically assault the business agent.

"Listen, you guys," the B.A. said, now visibly angry, too. "We had a hell of a time getting those breaks put in the contract. And now you guys aren't going to screw it up!"

It was quite true that the business agent had forgotten whom he was representing. He had let himself become a company enforcer. Our response to this, other than to vote him out of office the following year, was the worker's familiar one of ironic humor. Every time a controversy arose with the boss someone was sure to say, "Don't call the B.A. We've got enough people against us already."

To keep this from being misinterpreted, I must say that although workers on the job frequently find themselves in conflict with their own union officers, very few workers who are members of a trade union want to do away with their organization. We all recognize that there are things connected to our work that are beyond our jobs— industry-wide bargaining, for instance—and also that there is a need for a superstructure, a permanent bureaucracy, if you will, to administer jointly with the employer medical plans, vacations, pensions, etc. But as for the statement that good wages and good working conditions are the product of a strong trade union, it is the other way around. A strong trade union is the result of a strong rank and file, militant and unified, and that is created on the job through the relationships that work engenders among those who do it together. All trade unions function effectively in direct ratio to the strength of their rank-and-file workers. The workers come into being first, and the trade unions follow and build on them.

Having said this, how can one square this statement with the fact that many strong rank-and-file trade unions in America have gone into eclipse in recent years? The Rust Belt in midwest America provides us with numerous examples.

In 1963 over sixty percent of the mineral wealth of the world, including aggregates, found its way to America. The country had come out of World War II completely intact with its industrial capacity enhanced by the war effort. None of it was destroyed, either by invading troops or enemy bombers, and after a brief postwar pause it was switched over to manufacturing consumer products. Although most of these products were for domestic consumption, a sizable percentage of them were exported. The resulting profit from these exports so far surpassed the import cost of raw materials that by the early sixties the balance of payments was heavily in favor of the United States, and piling up. Every country in the world—well, perhaps not Switzerland—owed us money. As a companion to this situation America had also become an enormous market, almost as large as the rest of the world combined. Employment was universal, we were all working, and we were eager to spend the money we were earning. This market then became a political tool of American foreign policy, and it was put to use in a very deliberate way.

Classic Marxist dogma contended that capitalism was inevitably, historically doomed. Capitalists would, in their inherent need to expand, destroy each other fighting over markets wherever they sought them throughout the world. However, in a move that most Marxists still have not figured out, American capital offered America itself as a market, an enormous home for the expanding production of foreign goods and products. One very good example of this is sugar.

There are two sources of sugar, beets and cane, and one or the other can be grown just about anywhere in the world between permafrost in the north and Patagonia in the south. By 1963 America was offering sugar import quotas to twenty-seven different countries, essentially client states, about the world. At the time our own cane and beet growers, both on the mainland and in Hawaii, were subsidized in a price-support system that ranged around ten cents a pound. The twenty-seven foreign countries got not quite as much, but always considerably more than the price of sugar on the international commodities market, which at that time usually hovered somewhere around seven cents a pound. There was a competitive relationship here, of course, and the balance was precarious. These mostly small nations were constantly striving to increase their share of the American market at the expense of one another. One of these countries was Cuba. That is, until Castro came on the scene.

As client nations went, Cuba occupied a favored position vis-à-vis the United States in that they were at the head of the line to get the American sugar subsidy. It was not that they were a close neighbor or that we liked them especially; it was because a substantial part of the Cuban sugar industry was owned by American interests.

There was not much else going on in Cuba then. There was a large bauxite mining operation, exporting ore to be turned into aluminum in the United States, and the beginnings of a beef-cattle industry. After that it was whores, nightclubs, and gambling casinos, none of them industries to build a national economy around. Castro went east.

If there was one thing the Soviet Union and its satellite countries in Eastern Europe did not need, it was more sugar. They grew sugar beets from Poland east through the Crimea and the Caucasus and as far south as Bulgaria. Nevertheless, it was all Castro had to offer the Eastern Bloc in the way of trade goods in exchange for their support, so all these nations rearranged their agricultural priorities and let Cuba snuggle in. Two things happened as a result of this: first, the Cuban sugar allotment to the American market was eliminated. The Americans carefully redistributed it among their client states, rewarding those who had demonstrated the most enthusiasm and support for the current American foreign policy in their part of the world. The second thing that happened was that, after taking stock of our surpluses—for we had enormous stocks of sugar, too—the American government began dumping it on the international market, forcing the price, over a period of approximately six months, down to two-and-one-half cents a pound. The USSR had contracted to buy Cuban sugar for three times that amount well into the future. Sugar comes in bags. The Russians had been left holding one, and there was not very much they could do about it. It was not the first time the Russians were to be given a lesson in how to play hardball, American style, and it was not to be the last. But a reckoning was to come.

As time went on, offering up the American domestic market to the entry of foreign goods became an integral part of American foreign policy. Over the years, imports slowly supplanted goods that had been manufactured here. The demands of the Cold War and the loyalty of all those client states required that we provide them with an export market. The jobs lost to Americans at first were almost all blue collar, but, for a while, work was plentiful, and if a factory closed, a worker could usually find employment somewhere else. Finally, however, the Russians could sit back and have the last laugh watching us buy up a lot of stuff we could just as well have made for ourselves at home. By the mid-eighties the U.S. balance of trade deficit was over $100 billion a year and growing. Almost all the television sets and personal computers, along with forty percent of the automobiles in America, were made somewhere else. Most important, blue-collar unemployment had become endemic to our nation. Even regional industries, well represented by strong leadership in Congress, which historically maintained high tariffs to protect their own factories, such as the cotton goods trade in North and South Carolina, were overwhelmed. Whole factories were displaced, uprooted in many cases, and their stitching machines shipped somewhere south of the border, where they immediately took up production again. Most factory owners participated enthusiastically. They retained ownership, and their labor costs were one-quarter of what they had formerly been. They appeared not to care that each job destroyed by their move meant one less taxpayer supporting the common good, and very probably one more burden added to general welfare.

The rationale of those who extolled this policy was that while America was losing low-paying, unskilled, drudgery occupations, we were keeping and increasing highly skilled work that paid more money and offered a more imaginative and interesting way to spend our workday. Even if I concede that a job that requires someone to spend eight hours a day alone in a cubicle tending a computer is a lot of fun, which I won't, this is a dubious trade-off for the destruction of so much of America's industries and its blue-collar working class.

American foreign policy since President Harry Truman has remained essentially the same. Presidents have come and gone, some of them Democrats, others Republican, but our foreign policy has been consistent in placing as its primary focus the containment and eventual defeat of world communism under the leadership of the USSR. All things considered, it has been remarkably successful. If there was a winner in the Cold War, it certainly was not the Soviet Union. If the Cold War is over, however, the trade policies used to fight it remain in force, and now it is not only blue-collars who are suffering job losses. Via computer, information processing, bookkeeping and accounting, and similar work is being exported. For the American white-collar worker it is liable to be a very cold peace.

The broad terms given by the United States during the Cold War to define and solicit support for our side was that we, the forces of democracy, were in a death struggle with anti-democratic, totalitarian dictatorships. The definition of democracy was brief and specific: free speech and the right to vote. Despite the fact that the United States supported any number of regimes about the world that prohibited free speech and whose citizens, if they marked a ballot at all, found their choices limited to whomever was in power, American foreign policy worked toward objectives that were very well defined. In those countries we supported, no matter what their present democratic failings, U.S. foreign policy worked to establish a social democracy with a middle class of sufficient size and strength to take over and deny a successful revolution from a left-wing faction. Or a counter-revolution from the right wing. Right-wing regimes are oppressive; this makes them dangerous because of their susceptibility to left-wing revolutions. Left-wing revolutions, even those of a socialist nature, as opposed to communist, are categorically suspect because they might become resistant to American solutions to world problems. What America always sought was something comfortably in the middle.

The objective was clear, and the solution was simple: build up the middle class. All instincts toward democracy—free speech, free press, an honest vote, et cetera—are inherent in the middle class. Incipient democracy resides with them. All that is needed to change the various authoritarian governments about the world is to foster their middle class, and when it arrives at a certain size, democracy will break out, like sunshine. The American market has been the instrument of this attempted historical change, and the American blue-collar worker has, up to now, principally shouldered its cost. If it meant sacrificing American blue-collar worker's jobs to achieve this end, then that was the price that would have to be paid. Now it appears that the middle class is about to make a healthy contribution toward this effort by having a goodly portion of their jobs exported, too. Another segment of Karl Marx's thinking may be in error. On one level class warfare may not be inevitable. American blue-collar and white-collar workers could come together and bond over the same objective, saving their jobs. If the two classes do become united, the task ahead of them is formidable: how to change America's combined economic and foreign policy.

One finds irony in abundance in Karl Marx. Sarcasm, rage, and outrage, too. For such a clinically analytic thinker he was a passionate man. His primary vision was that the forces of capitalism would destroy themselves in a final death struggle for the markets of the world. One wonders: Were he alive today, what would his comment be? How ironic that capitalism has turned Marx upside down, stood him on his head. Instead of seeking out and fighting over the markets of the world, capitalism has turned America into the biggest market of them all.

And the balance of trade deficit? According to the last year for which we have complete data, America imported more than $100 billion worth of stuff *more* than we sold abroad, that is, exported. And those nations, like Japan, which continue to collect all those American greenbacks with pictures of our dead presidents on them for the goods they send us, what is their response to all this? Actually, these nations don't have much choice other than to continue on with things as they now are. Otherwise, where are they going to send all that stuff they continue to manufacture?

CHAPTER SEVEN

Tip That Drum, Tote That Bale

Abale of cotton weighs 500 pounds. A fifty-gallon steel drum of oil usually weighs in at somewhere between 450 and 500 pounds, so their weights are about the same. Along with all other commodities, much of this cargo is now loaded aboard ship in containers and sent overseas without any longshoreman touching it. But there are still a lot of bales and drums stowed by hand in various seaports around the world.

Two longshoremen traditionally work together handling both of these cargoes. For some reason, personal taste, I suppose, I have always found drums easier to stow aboard ship than cotton. However I am in the minority among longshoremen. Neither cotton nor steel drums are anybody's favorite cargo to work, but when a guy is picking up a job and he has a choice between the two, most everyone will pick cotton.

Longshoremen do not really lift—pick up—either of these commodities, of course. After the winch-driver brings the cotton into the hatch, usually three bales at a time on a wire sling, the men place themselves at either end of a bale and, using their cargo hooks, roll the bales one at a time back under the deck and into the farthest reaches of the hold. We call it flooring off. Each cotton bale ends up flat, snuggled up tight against the next bale, one high, until the gang works its way out to the square of the open hatch, where the sunlight is. Once there, the winch-driver lands the bales right in place, which takes only two men to help guide them to rest, meaning all the other members of the gang can sit down and take a break. When the square of the hatch is filled the guys grab their hooks and go back to flooring off again, rolling the bales way back under the deck to the far corners of the hold and working their way out once more toward the open hatch again.

Working steel drums is similar to working bales of cotton in that you can flop the drums over on their side and then roll them back to where you have to stow them. But then you have to stand them up again. This constitutes the major difference in stowing the two cargos. Drums are never stowed on their sides, but cotton is always packed in flat. After you have put a bale of cotton in place you simply leave it there and walk away from it, get another bale. Drums, wherever you load them, you have to stand up. Meaning, unlike cotton, you have to handle them twice.

"I don't like drums," is a typical comment. "You have to handle them too much." So why am I—and a minority of other longshoremen—being perverse in preferring drums to cotton?

First, 500 pounds is 500 pounds, but there are different ways of working it. Flopping steel drums can be a snap. Tipping a drum, so you can flop it on its side, is done by placing one hand on a neighboring drum and pushing against it while pulling your drum toward you with your other arm. It does not come easy, but a reasonably strong man can do it. If you want to be slick, you can nudge your drum a little bit. The liquid inside it slops around. When it slops in your direction, give the drum a pull. The drum will come easier. When you have the drum supported at a tilt, the weight resting on a small arc of its bottom edge, you can wheel it around, flop it in the direction of where you want it to go, and give it a little kick. Drums are round. They roll easily. Try kicking a bale of cotton. The rub comes, of course, when you have to stand the drum up. It takes two men to do it. It is a tough lift and they have to give it all their strength, but it is worth it. At least you are not in some other hatch shoving and pulling that cotton around. All cargo aboard ship has to be stowed tight. When stowing cotton, if the Walking-Boss comes down into the hatch and walks around on top to the bales, they better not wiggle.

"Hey, you guys," he'll yell, standing on some bale and rocking it back and forth under him by shifting his weight. "You guys aren't stowing this cotton tight enough. All you guys get up off your asses and get over here and take up this slack."

When this happens the whole gang has to turn-to and go to work. If you have been working on and off—four men working at full blast to keep the hook moving so the others can take a break—everybody has to get up and go to work to make things right. Just one loose bale can mean rearranging the whole damned hatch, because when you close the gap on one bale, it leaves another hole behind it so you have to snug up that bale, which leaves another hole, and so on. Drums, on the other hand, fit neatly into each offset, nesting right up against each other. No Walking-Boss is going to make them wiggle. Drums have another advantage over cotton. When you have the drum tilted toward you and are holding it balanced on the bottom edge, one man can roll it rather easily, on edge, eight or ten feet anyway. What this means is that your range of stowage back under the combing away from the square of the hatch is vastly improved. Long before he works his way back to daylight one man can roll his drum on edge to its final rest and slam it in place without having to flop it over, roll it, and then stand it back up again. Don't tell me that drums aren't better than cotton!

People who work with drums all the time get very good at it, as it is with all work. The best drum-men I ever saw were two teamsters down-loading drums off the bed of a truck to the dock. The teamster on the truck—actually a flatbed trailer—was flopping the drum over on its side and rolling it down a ramp to the dock toward his partner. His partner was a good fifty feet away. He was receiving the steel drums on the roll, standing them up and nesting them against each other in rows about twelve drums wide. All by himself! But he had a tool, a spud, a five-foot length of two-by-four whittled down to a flat, wedgelike shape at one end. By the time the drum got to the bottom of the ramp it was going at a pretty good clip, straight toward the man on the dock. He waited, the blunt end of the spud held in both hands waist-high with the wedge end resting flat on the floor pointed toward the oncoming drum. When the drum got to him, he let it roll up the spud just below the top rim of the drum until it got about knee-high. Then, lifting his end of the spud quickly, he flipped the drum upright. It slid into its place in the row right next to the previous drum. Then he turned around to receive the next drum, which was already coming at him. I was pretty good at handling drums, but I never got *that* good.

When you work, work at hard physical labor, and you encounter someone else somewhere else doing the same job you do, you always check them out. How good are they at it? And you always think you can do it better. But not those teamsters. I don't know who the first man was who believed, I mean was totally convinced, that he could whittle one end of a length of two-by-four into the shape of a wedge and let someone else roll a five hundred pound drum full of oil at him, and then, by thrusting the wedge end of that two-by-four under that drum when it came at him and giving it a quick flip, could stand that 500-pound drum upright, right alongside another drum, and make rows out of them—well, that man was something else. He had to have a lot of confidence in himself and that spud. Stand me up and roll a 500-pound steel drum at me, and I would have to think it over. Those drums were coming at that teamster standing on the dock at a fast clip. At the last minute I think I would have broke and run, dropped the two-by-four spud, and leaped for the rafters, or climbed a wall in panic. But somewhere along the line someone decided he could do it. And he did do it. He changed the way drums were downloaded off a truck forever. At least until they were placed on pallet boards and moved around with a forklift truck.

All workers perfect techniques for doing their jobs faster, easier, and more efficiently. And then someone figures out an even better way and those original heroes are forgotten, lost from memory forever. Who invented the forklift truck? I don't know, and I drove one for years. It was probably put together by a committee. Will they be forgotten, too? It appears they already have been.

CHAPTER EIGHT

The Depression

I am of an age that I remember the Great Depression of the 1930s. It was aptly named. Foremost among other things it was very depressing, especially the winters.

Don't let anyone tell you it doesn't get cold in California. I remember a lot of frigid, foggy days in the San Joaquin Valley when the temperature never got much above freezing, and the sun did not come out for a week at a time. I remember especially one three-week period spanning Christmas and the New Year spent in a thin-walled little house in a small town by the railroad tracks where the family waited for a winter vegetable deal, probably cauliflower, to materialize. It never did start up and produce jobs. Every day freight trains going north and south would pass by, covered with hobos making their way somewhere, anywhere, men on the bum. My mother dared not hang out laundry on the clothesline overnight. It would be gone in the morning.

Before this account gets too grim, however, let me say that I do not ever remember having gone hungry. All credit goes to my mother. She kept everything together, most of all the family. My father was always off somewhere else, sometimes running a packing shed, more often working on one. He would return to where we were, pack tomatoes for a few weeks, if that was the commodity currently providing work, and then be gone again. Sometimes it was to Arizona or Texas, and winter lettuce. Once it was to Mexico, way down, far south, where they grew cantaloupes in February. Then one time he went off somewhere and he did not come back. We always knew vaguely where he was, or where he had been. Fruit-tramps kept track of each other. Someone could be relied on to tell us when they had seen him last. There were occasions, rare, when he would appear suddenly for an afternoon. We three kids might be then taken out to a drive-in for cheeseburgers and malts, and deposited back home before dark. My brother and I once spent three weeks with my father in Phoenix, Arizona. It was July, very hot, and we saw very little of him because he was working late every night on a melon job. On our way back to California in search of my mother, who was packing peaches and with whom my sister had remained, my father on the spur of the moment detoured up to the Grand Canyon. My brother and I were properly impressed with its vastness and depth, but what really got our attention were the flying squirrels leaping out of one pine tree and gliding hundreds of yards into the branches of another. From the age of about seven, however, until I was an adult, my father was not a big part of my life.

Winters got so tough my mother finally gathered up us three kids and made her way to San Francisco and went on relief. President

Roosevelt's New Deal was providing a subsistence level of support to all who needed it, and we got in line.

After all the small towns I had lived in, San Francisco was a new world to me. In a small town we three kids showed up at a small school and enrolled as strangers, most often in midsemester. Even if I had been there the previous year, I knew no one because I had not been there long enough to get to know anyone. Sometimes the teacher would introduce me to the class, sometimes not. I would take a seat at a desk in the rear of the room and fidget while everyone turned and stared at me. The other kids weren't unfriendly, they just occupied a world in which they had all known each other since birth, or since the previous September, which was approximately the same thing to them. I was simply not a part of their world. In the school-yard at noon, I ate my lunch alone. At recess I played alone, or stood alone and watched other kids noisily jostle and shove each other to get their turn on the rings or the slide. If I got in line to climb the ladder to go down the slide, they jostled in front of me and they jostled behind me, but they very politely let me have my turn.

In those days a number of small towns in California openly practiced segregation. In some old building on the other side of the railroad tracks, the black kids and the Mexican kids were carefully shunted aside educationally. Once my brother and sister and I ended up in one of those institutions, until my mother took time off work to go down and raise hell and get us transferred across town to go to school back with the white folk. In towns too small to have more than one school, we all ended up together. I remember only a few black kids in those situations, and they were pretty much integrated, sitting wherever in the classroom they wanted and taking full part in all the activities, probably because there were so few of them. The Mexicans, however, were aliens—they even spoke in a foreign tongue—

and no attempt was made to keep them from gravitating to the rear of the class, where, upon entry, I ended up. I wasn't one of them, but the Mexicans were friendly to me. I even learned a little Spanish. *Besa mi culo* means "kiss my ass."

Summertime, as it was to everyone connected to the crops, was a time of plenty. For the fruit-tramps the living wasn't easy, but there was an abundance of work and of course a variety of ripe fruit to eat. Sometimes we camped out. I remember sleeping in a tent by a river the entire month of July three years in a row while my mother packed peaches in a packing shed in town. We kids went swimming every day, and got acquainted with the other campers, the vanguard, the very first, of the Okies. The following winter it was back to San Francisco one more time.

George Orwell has described being down and out in Paris and London as nothing less than an exhausting ordeal, a scramble just to stay alive. I would hesitate to describe those same years in San Francisco using language that severe. Poverty as the result of unemployment was endemic to the city, of course, as it was to the rest of America, and my mother must have been sorely pressed at times to construct different menus out of the government handout of canned beef and cornmeal. She must indeed have looked forward to summer. When everyone is in the same boat, however, the leveling that takes place among everyone, although not exhilarating, enables one to jettison some of the social burden. Envy, for instance. What is there to envy? Someone else's canned beef and cornmeal?

Some people felt stigmatized by being out of work and on relief and unquestionably had a harder time accepting it than others did. I remember a long line of patient people, ourselves among them, strung out in an alley south of Market Street, huddling against the wind. We were waiting for handouts of a bushel basket of food from some agency or another. The fresh, newly woven wooden baskets had distinctive markings with blue trim and red handles, and I remember vividly one family of a father, mother, and two children, a boy and a girl not much older than my ten years. When they finally received their basket they immediately distributed the contents—the apples, the oranges, the cheap hardrock candy, the cans of pork and beans—among the four of them. The groceries rapidly disappeared inside their coats and jackets, and when they were left with the empty basket, the mother cast it down to the alley's asphalt and thrust a foot at the container in an attempt to crush it. She was quickly joined by the rest of the family. The father, caving in one side of the basket with a worn work boot, held it down while the rest of the family got in their licks. The boy finished it off, jumping up and down and landing with both feet on the hated object, leaving the basket a mass of bright, new, splintered wood marked with dirty footprints. Then he hurried off to catch up with the rest of the family, who were rapidly fleeing down the alley away from the symbolic remnants of their poverty and shame.

Unlike in the small towns, however, we were never made to feel we were intruders in San Francisco. The schools were so big that when I enrolled the teacher accepted me as if I were merely transferring from one class to another. At lunchtime we all sat on long benches around the edge of the schoolyard, throwing the remnants of our corned beef sandwiches to the waiting seagulls, strutting around the asphalt just beyond our reach. After the gulls devoured our scraps, they took off for other schoolyards farther inland. When they came back in a fly-over toward the ocean, just before the bell rang summoning us back to class, we all ran for cover to avoid being hit by big gobs of splattering white seagull shit. The gulls were returning our lunch.

At the end of the second day of school I fell in with a group of boys who took me with them to the back room of a large commercial bakery where we scraped out and cleaned pie tins. In return we got to eat the pies too broken and fragmented by the automatic baking process for the route men to sell to the countless little corner stores throughout the city. After gorging ourselves on pie, we made our way to the local park and, along with other boys, were organized into two sandlot football teams by a couple of bigger kids. They picked the sides by the authority of being fifteen-year-olds. One fifteen-year-old had the football, the other owned the only helmet among the group. They both played quarterback, naturally. I was picked almost last by the kid with the helmet and placed in the line, of course, not the backfield. But I caught a pass he threw me, which I fumbled just as I crossed the goal line, causing one hell of an argument about whether it was a touchdown or not. There was a lot of angry shoving back and forth among the members of both teams, but there were no fights. Our side prevailed for some reason, and it was a touch-down. On the following kickoff, however, I was slammed into, smashed, and leveled three times before I got even halfway down-field. But what the hell, that just told me everybody knew who I was. I had been chosen next to last when they selected the teams. The next time we played football, I was picked third and placed specifi-cally at right end.

Following that second winter in San Francisco we returned to fruit-tramping again in late spring. I expected that we would be back the next fall, but my mother landed a winter job packing oranges in Southern California, and I was an adult before I saw San Francisco again; but I never forgot it. There was an air of confidence in the city even though we were in the middle of the Depression. The previous summer had been the time of the General Strike. There had been beatings and shootings and tear-gassing by cops and National Guard troops all along the waterfront, but the longshoremen, the seamen, the teamsters, and all the rest of labor had come through it intact. They had survived and they had won and they were modestly triumphant. That waterfront was the same one I found employment on twenty-five years later.

CHAPTER NINE

Working Women

Acouple of years after the split between my mother and father became permanent, my mother acquired a companion, another fruit-tramp named Ernie. My mother and Ernie lasted about three years, and then she threw him out. After Ernie, as far as I know, there were no other men in my mother's life.

Ernie was a boozer. I would not call him a complete drunk, but Ernie always needed liquor to get through the day. We three kids did not particularly like him, but Ernie was not all that bad. Occupying the role of stepfather was something new for him, and he must have found it a trial. However, he never whacked us (my mother would probably have laid him out if he had) and he used to take us places sometimes.

My most outstanding memory of Ernie was the time he took us to the San Diego Zoo. We drove over from the Imperial Valley and arrived there in late morning. It was a weekday, and the zoo was deserted. We quickly made our way to the elephant compound. We particularly wanted to see the elephants. We three kids had our collective bag of peanuts, and Ernie had his pint of bourbon, which he would occasionally tip up to take a swig. The elephants, four of them, were separated from us spectators by a deep moat, but the absence of a chain-link fence and the enormity of the huge animals made them undeniably *right there*. They could almost reach across and touch us with their long trunks.

We took turns tossing our peanuts across to them. Between tenor-like roars they would deftly sweep up a peanut with the tip of their digital, prehensile-like trunks and deposit it in their mouths. And then one peanut I threw fell short. It landed about halfway down the far, sloping bank of the moat. A wasted peanut, everyone thought, and then one elephant, placing his forefeet on the very edge of the moat, reached way down with his trunk and snatched it up. Then it became a contest between us three kids to see how far an elephant was willing to reach down into the moat to retrieve a peanut. The great beasts, not only intelligent but very nimble, would balance themselves on their back feet, place their front feet a foot or so down into the moat, and reach halfway down the slope to pick up the morsel. We never did find out how far they could stretch because we ran out of peanuts.

When the peanuts stopped coming, the elephants, the four of them, lined up, roared a bit, and waved their trunks at us, demanding more nuts. At a loss, we kids just stood there, unwilling to deceive them further by waving back.

"You want some more peanuts?" Ernie exclaimed, slipping his pint into a rear pocket. "I'll give you some more peanuts." Ernie reached down and, no less nimbly than the elephants, whipped up a small rock and let it fly. He hit the largest animal right in the center of his forehead. The elephant blinked and let out a roar. He did not even search the ground around him. He knew he hadn't been hit by a peanut. He let out another roar, louder than the first, and waved his trunk around in a decidedly agitated manner. Ernie gathered up a handful of small rocks and pebbles, and began pelting the whole herd. Very quickly the roars became deafening. Just a few yards across the moat from us, four enormous beasts were threatening us with mayhem. And then the four of them backed off and bunched together, facing each other in the center of their compound. It looked as if they might be gathering themselves for a running jump at us. We three kids cowered in retreat, looking around for a tree to climb, a place to hide, anything. Ernie had a pretty good sidearm, and he continued bouncing pebbles off the four of them. Then the elephants suddenly grew silent and began to gather in a circle.

My mother was the first to figure out what was happening. Behind us, she broke out laughing. "They're old circus elephants," she said. "They're from a circus." Sure enough, she was right. The elephants were slowly ambling around in a circle, each holding on to the tail of the one in front of him with his trunk. Every now and then one of them would raise a trunk and let out a shriek. Old Ernie the elephant trainer kept them going with an occasional well-placed pebble. Then, animal keepers, yard people, and other zoo employees started showing up to see what all the commotion was about, and we got the hell out of there. My brother and I gathered up a handful of pebbles and small rocks, hoping to get Ernie over to the area where they kept the big cats. We wanted to see what he could do with the lions. We never found out. Ernie got too juiced to throw straight. Ernie wasn't such a bad guy. He simply couldn't jack himself to get in line and march around in circles.

My mother worked all her life. She, like most fruit-tramp women, ended up single. Even those women who remained married were single a lot of the time, with their husbands working in the melons, and they, hundreds of miles away sometimes, packing peaches, or pears, or tomatoes. In the fall the married couples might assemble again, packing tomatoes together somewhere on the California coast, but the melon harvest could easily run well up into October, and the packing of honeydews, Persians, and Cranshaw melons sometimes lasted until almost Christmas. If you worked on one of those jobs, it was only a scant four months or so until you started all over again when the first cantaloupes began ripening once more in southern Texas.

I think my mother was like a lot of American working women who end up alone in middle age. She rather liked it. After we kids were gone, she had only herself to take care of, and no man to answer to. Unquestionably she felt lonely at times, but I also think she felt free. There was plenty of work for fruit-tramps during and after World War II, and the money she made was hers to spend alone on herself for a change. Between jobs she and small groups of her female fruit-tramp friends might drive to Reno or Las Vegas for a weekend of petty gambling, a luxury she had never let herself afford before.

In the final analysis, work, I think, has had a liberating effect on American women. But if a woman marries and has a family, freedom only comes with age. It is a rare blue-collar male now working forty hours a week who can support a family on just his wages alone. Wives have had to step in and find a job if the family is going to have any kind of extra money. There may still be blue-collar families around where the woman of the house is solely a housewife and mother, but I do not know of any. In my rather large circle of acquaintances, all the women work. Their only time off has been when they had a child, and that is certainly no vacation. And it is not for very long; after a short time the kid is in nursery school and mom is back at the old grind. With time on the job comes seniority and, usually, pay raises, and many middle-aged couples and singles find themselves with surplus money to spend for the first time in their lives. I have noticed, however, that a lot of that money is siphoned off by their now-adult children, many of whom are still living at home.

When women first came to work as longshoremen on the San Francisco waterfront, they were not welcome. Longshorewomen came into existence by law, by affirmative action. They were legislated into what had been an exclusively male occupation. Since I had had the experience of working with women on an equal basis as a fruit-tramp, I did not have the difficulty most longshoremen had in accepting them. The men's complaints were many, and not all of them were without merit.

"They'll never make it down here," was the almost universal verdict. "How are they going to work coffee? Or cotton? Or lash down vans?"

"How are we going to work 'on–and-off?' " was another complaint. "They'll never be able to keep up. We're going to lose all our working conditions. They'll never be any good down here." But women made it, and now they are employed in longshore in almost all the ports in America.

Automation and the container came to the waterfront about the same time as women, and it unquestionably helped them because it made some jobs easier. It helped a lot of men, too, many of whom had come to longshoring later in life and had not built up enough seniority to get themselves on a skill-board where the living was easy. They were flopping on coffee, cotton, and other hard jobs, going home from the dispatch without work. But automation eliminated a lot of the easy work along with the hard, and many men felt threats coming from both directions.

As for hard work, some women can do anything, even work sack coffee. I had heard about this one young lady long before I saw her in action. She was working extra, catching jobs when there were a lot of ships in port and not enough regular longshoremen to cover all the work. Since casuals, as we call them, get the jobs that are left over, which no longshoreman will take if he has a choice, that means hard work, and this young lady was reputed to take on anything. She was even reputed to be rather good at sack coffee, all seventy kilos of it, all 154 pounds. Well, half of it anyway: there is always someone else on the other end of the sack.

I finally encountered this young woman when I first switched over to working nights. I was driving a forklift on the dock in a gang, taking away loads of coffee being palletized down in our hatch. It was my plan to go aboard ship the first chance I got and see how she did her work. I got my chance sooner than I expected; I was shop steward in the gang and very shortly we had a work stoppage.

When the loads of coffee stopped coming out of the hold, I answered a summons to go aboard ship. The winch-driver had hung the hook, and the gang boss and the walking boss were leaning over the coaming, staring down into the hatch. I joined them but I remained silent. I had a rule: as shop steward I did not talk to anybody until I first talked to the men doing the work—and one woman, in this instance.

"What's happening?" I yelled down into the hold.

"We got only five men," someone answered, meaning they were working short-handed.

The young lady, it turned out, was black. Black was nothing exceptional; half the waterfront was black, but she did not look like someone who could throw coffee sacks for an indefinite period of time. A nondescript young woman of medium height, perhaps a bit stocky under a pair of loose-fitting coveralls, she was sitting alone on a stack of pallet boards down below.

"We been carrying the gang and we're not going to do it any longer," one man down below said. The other three men nodded in agreement. All the men in the gang appeared to be of one mind.

A coffee discharge gang worked six men in three teams of two each. They worked one hour on, a half-hour off, in rotation. When you pump out coffee for an hour, you need that half-hour just to re-cover, gain back your strength. The guys had worked for hour. As far as they were concerned, it was now someone else's problem.

"Where's her partner?" I asked the gang boss.

"She had one," the walking boss said, "but she ran him off."

"I don't blame her a damn bit," the gang boss said. "He wasn't packing his weight. She had to set up all the sacks, drag all the pallet-boards, everything. . . . She was doing all the work."

"Get another man from the Hiring Hall," I said to the gang boss.

"Can't."

"Why not?"

"Ain't got none."

"Try the warehouse local."

"Ain't got none there, either."

"Try their East Bay Hiring Hall," I said.

"Already did."

"Well?"

"They can't get anyone here before lunch time." Obviously, there were a lot of ships in the port. I looked at my watch. Lunch was damn near three hours off.

"All right," the walking boss said. "I want to see some coffee come out of this hatch. Otherwise, I'm going to have to fire the gang."

Hell, sometimes a man's got to do what a man's got to do, just to keep things moving in this world.

"Gaffer, go down on the dock and drive lift for me, will you?" I asked the gang boss. "I'll be right back." I went out to the car, opened the trunk, and rummaged through the box in which I kept all my old gloves and work equipment. I found what I was looking for way down in the bottom of the box underneath a pair of caulked boots I wore when I traveled up north and worked the log-rafts in Oregon. There it was, my old sack-hook. That sack-hook had been given to me by Cecil, an old longshoreman I knew, when he retired. It had been a while since I had used it—it was even a little rusty—but it was the best sack-hook I had ever worked with. It had five small tines in a row, built into a slight angle with the shaft, and it fit into the palm of your hand just right. It almost made you *want* to work coffee. Well, no, not really. No sack-hook is that good.

The girl was morose to a point just short of being constantly angry. After we flopped down a pallet-board, I hooked into a sack of coffee along a seam and spun it around, setting it up for the both of us. She threw her sack okay, packing her half of the weight, maybe even a little more. Before I could reach for another sack, she had one already set up for us. She was very quick. We pitched that sack, and I set up the next. We went on working that way, she setting up a sack, I doing the next. Between loads she would lean against the coffee with her arms folded and stare off into space. She had a funny look-ing little old hook, which, it seemed, she had to sink into the sack just right or it would slip out on her. After about the eighth load, the winches broke down for a little while—thank God—and we got a short rest.

"My name is Ralph Waldo Emerson," I said to her. "What's yours?"

"You ain't no Ralph Waldo Whomsoever," she said accusingly. "That ain't your name. I heard what they call you."

"Hmmmm. Is that so?" She took her stance again, leaning against the coffee, staring out at nothing. Finally, the winches came back on and we went back to work. I set up the first sack, and we threw it on the pallet-board. She reached for the second sack, and then paused.

"My name is Billie," she said, grudgingly.

It had been a couple of years since I had worked coffee. When our half-hour break came I was, frankly, exhausted. I flopped down out of the way on a coffee sack. Billie had also broken a sweat. She sat down on another sack of coffee a little distance away from me, panting and sucking in air, too. She was far enough away from me to be alone, but close enough so that, somehow, we were taking our break together. As a partner on coffee she was okay. She was, in fact, very good. She was young, and strong, but that in itself was not enough to successfully work coffee for an entire shift. She had come to understand the two cardinal facts of how to do hard work: how to pace yourself and save your strength, and how to exert the minimum effort to accomplish the task at hand.

"How come you doin' this?" she said suddenly.

"Doing what?"

"You the forklift driver in this gang. How come you down here working coffee?"

"The walking boss was going to fire the gang. I'm filling in. You'll have a new partner after lunch."

"Jis' my luck. I hope he's better than the last one."

"Get yourself a partner, Billie. Somebody you can work with. A good partner is awfully important on the waterfront. If you have a good partner you can handle just about any kind of work they can throw at you. The gangs will be glad to see you show up on the job, and the walking bosses will leave you alone."

When we went back to work it was the last hour before lunch. When we had about twenty minutes left in the hour, I stopped her just as she was reaching for the next sack.

"Let me see your hook, Billie," I said. She stopped and just stared at me. Finally, reluctantly, she passed me her hook. When I took it, I pressed the handle of my hook into the palm of her hand. "Try that on for size," I said.

We worked three more loads and then it was time for lunch. As we stood by the ladder, she turned my hook over, back and forth in her hand. "Man, this is some hook," she said, offering it back to me.

"I'm the second generation to use that hook," I said. "You're the third."

"What do you mean?"

"It's your hook."

"You mean it?" She was incredulous. A good hook is a small treasure.

"It's your hook, Billie." For the first time, she smiled.

"Thank you, Waldo."

After the lunch break I was back sitting on my forklift—thank God. I reflected on Billie. If American women have seen a host of new jobs open up to them under affirmative action, they have also lost a few things. One of my first jobs as a fifteen-year-old was on a packing shed lifting boxes of pears off their packing benches for the women. Under President Roosevelt's New Deal, the Department of Labor had initiated a thirty-two-pound limit on what working women could be made to lift. It created a job for me. A box of pears weighed fifty-five pounds. I would run up and down the line of packers and set off a full box whenever a woman packer raised her hand and signaled to me. I do not know whatever happened to that thirty-two-pound law, but it is no longer in force. If you do not believe me, ask Billie.

My own personal opinion is that Billie should not have been there, down in that hatch throwing sacks of coffee. They were too heavy for her. Sooner or later she was going to break down physically under a steady routine of too-heavy work. Just as strongly, I am also of the opinion that I should not have been down there lifting that weight either, nor should have any other longshoreman who, when he retires, invariably does so with a bad back resulting from hopelessly damaged discs. To organize work into a series of onerous workloads of whatever kind, and to mandate that workers must accept that workload, is to sentence workers to end their lives as cripples. It does not make sense to enclose seventy kilos of coffee in one sack. It could weigh half that. The same goes for the weights of any number of other commodities.

When women entered the workforce on the waterfront I thought that they might bring a new approach to old work practices. I even argued that possibility with my fellow longshoremen. I was wrong. Nothing much changed because of gender. Certainly women coming to work on the waterfront had nothing approaching the impact that automation and the seagoing van had. Billie may have been the third generation to use that sack-hook, but she did not use it for very long. A short time after I gave my hook to her, coffee began showing up aboard ship already palletized. We lowered forklifts into the hold and drove the pallets of coffee under the hook. A couple of years after that, working coffee as a job disappeared entirely for us. The coffee was there. But it was inside vans and we never even saw it, much less touched it. San Francisco longshoremen, of whatever sex, retired their sack-hooks forever. That coffee, however, was being lifted somewhere else.

Longshoremen in the coffee ports of South America were known as a group to be just about the strongest longshoremen in the world. They took the sack of coffee, balanced it on their shoulders, walked it back under the combing of the hatch to wherever they were stowing it, and then dropped it in place. Sometimes they had to pack it uphill if they were high-piling the sacks. These longshoremen were proud of their strength, and rightly so, because it was what gave them power over their work. They used their unique strength to extract from their employers the highest wages and the best working conditions of any other workers in the countries in which they labored.

Most of what I know of longshore work in other parts of the world has come from what American and foreign seamen have told me. From on-and-off practices in Scandinavia (one hour on and one hour off, usually; all younger men down in the hold) to the number of men in a gang in Manila (twenty-four) and India (uncountable), seamen have been my best source of information. With the advent of the Industrial Revolution and its accompanying worldwide trade, workers have responded as best they could to the work they did. In the Orient, longshoremen work cheap, but they create as many jobs as possible for their sons, nephews, and brothers. In America and Europe, they take care of themselves by working their asses off when they are young to shorten their workday (which is what on-and-off essentially is) and then progress to an easier job when they are older, say, driving a forklift. The South American longshoremen had to be unique in the world. While everyone else who worked for a living was trying to reduce the weight they were compelled to pick up, they wanted to keep it. They were maintaining control over their work by making certain that no one else could do it. One could almost say that there was a symbiotic relationship between those longshoremen and seventy kilos of weight. It would be interesting to find out which came first, the heavy coffee sack or the strong men who came into existence to work it.

My sources of information about how work is performed in foreign ports has slowly dried up. The fewer and fewer seamen I encounter now tell me they do not know, they cannot tell, how many longshoremen are employed in any given operation. Almost all cargo is in sea-vans now, the ship is in port for only a few hours usually, and everything is moving too fast to make an accurate study. They do not see the strong physical specimens they once did in South American ports, they say. The coffee to be loaded is already in vans there, just as it is discharged in vans here, and there appears to be no need for them, at least on the waterfront. Did they follow the vans out to the plantation to work the coffee there? I do not think so. I am told they do see an occasional woman on the docks, however.

If Billie could work coffee, she was probably capable of working just about any cargo. However, there are blue-collar jobs in industry that all except the very strongest women simply cannot do. When the luck of the draw deals an average woman one of these jobs, it leads to problems. A couple of years after working with Billie on coffee, I encountered one of these problems on a container ship.

On a container ship the vans to be loaded below deck are not lashed to the ship or to each other; they simply fit into slots. On deck, however, the vans have to be lashed down and secured to withstand the pitching and rolling of the vessel during the three weeks or so that it takes to cross one of the world's oceans. Vans may weigh thirty tons and be stacked five high, and the swing back and forth may achieve forty degrees as the ship rolls from one side to the other. The vans have to be secured to withstand these forces, tied down, that is, with lengths of chain, or cable, or long steel rods. The newer vessels use rods, and they are heavy. They have to be lifted and hooked into the bottom of the third row of vans up from the deck, a reach of about sixteen to eighteen feet. After the rod is in place it is tightened down with a heavy turnbuckle.

I was driving a tractor, meaning I was towing an empty trailer on the dock in preparation to receive a van to be discharged by the shore crane from the container ship I was working. It was the start of the shift, and as the longshoremen filed up the gangplank, I noticed that there were two women in their company. At the start of the operation a container ship can be easy work. All you do is disconnect the lashings and let them fall. When the containers are discharged down to the bare deck, things change. In this instance all the incoming Frisco vans were above deck, so as soon as the deck was cleared, the crane began loading outgoing vans back aboard ship.

Everything went smoothly at first. We had six tractor drivers for our crane. When I pulled under the hook, the crane driver landed a van on my trailer. The two dockmen secured the container at all four corners of my trailer with steel pins, and I drove off and parked the van in the yard. Then I would hook up to an empty chassis and get in line at the crane again. Once, in response to an outsider's question, "What is your job like?" I told him to go out, get into his car, and drive around the block for eight hours. After driving tractor for a while, that is pretty much how it feels.

Loading is the same as discharging. You move forward slowly, joke with the pinmen when they come by to free your van, and then, after the crane takes away your container, make another round and take up the conversation again. I had just been elected vice-president of our local, so the two pinmen, older men whom I had known for many years, were giving me a hard time.

"Okay, we voted for you," the larger of the pinmen said, standing beside my cab. "So, now that you're in office, I guess you're going to start wearing a suit and tie to work, huh?" The crane was not moving. His partner, who had a game leg, came lurching around from the other side of the tractor.

"Is it like we said, Al?" Gimpy said to his partner. "Is he already drunk with power?" The vice-president is just about the lowest man on the totem pole in our union, so he was having a joke.

The crane still had not moved. We three continued, discussing the weather, how despondent we were over world affairs, and the deplorable absence of supervisors coming around to tell us how to do our job. Then I noticed the walking boss coming down the gangplank with the two women longshoremen following him. He brought the two women over to where we were.

"You two go aboard ship and lash vans," he said to Gimpy and his partner. "I'm putting these two girls to work here pulling pins." Evidently the crane had stopped taking vans aboard ship because the lashers had not completed their work. The heavy steel rods had unquestionably got the better of the two young women. Neither Gimpy, his partner, nor I said a word. We just stared at the man.

"All right, get moving!" the walking boss said, finally.

"I'll tell you what," said Gimpy. "Why don't you go get fu . . ."

"You can't do that," I said, interrupting Gimpy, trying to keep him out of trouble.

"Why not?" the walker demanded, turning on me. I was going out on a limb, exceeding my authority. This dispute should properly be handled by a business agent, not a mere vice-president. Oh, well.

"These men are dockmen," I said. "They don't have to go aboard ship."

"These men were dispatched as lashers, like everybody else. I can put them to work wherever I want."

"If these women can't do the work, why don't you call the Hiring Hall and get replacements?" I said. The walking boss looked uncomfortable. Finally, he turned his attention from us to the two young women.

"Come with me," he said. The three of them took off together.

I had heard that the stevedore companies had told their bosses to tread carefully where women workers were concerned. They were being overly cautious, afraid of being charged with sexual discrimination. Thirty minutes after the walking boss left us, two more men came from the hiring hall and went aboard ship to join the other lashers. Later I saw the two women down at the far end of the dock. The walker had put them to work sorting the cones that are placed in the corners of the vans to seat and lock the succeeding layers of containers that are stacked, one on top of the other, on deck, a make-work activity to keep the women busy.

Nothing of note happened on the pier after that, except that every time I showed up under the crane with a van, Gimpy and his partner came to attention, saluted, and then bowed down and chanted, "We are unworthy, we are unworthy." Sometimes the guys never let up. For months afterward, every time I ran into the holdmen in the coffee gang with whom Billie and I had worked, they called me Waldo.

The problem the two women presented, and others like it, was solved in the Port of San Francisco by the longshoremen themselves, somewhat in the manner of their South American brothers. Only strong young men ended up lashing vans aboard ship. They volunteered for the job and they worked as a crew. Their reward was that they lashed vans, and that was their job, nothing else. Between lashing rows of vans they went to the coffee shack and played cards, listened to the radio, or did whatever else they chose to do. When another tier of vans was ready, they turned out and worked with a vengeance. It all worked out; the crane moved smoothly instead of by fits and starts, the work got done, and sometimes the lashers even got a two-hour lunch. The lashers were the last to go home, however. Long after the last van had been put aboard and we tractor drivers had parked our rigs, the lashers were still finishing up the ship. If he was a smart walking boss, he gave them an extra half-hour overtime to make sure he got the same crew back next time. That is, to keep them from picking up a job at another pier.

When you put men and women together, sex always comes up. Or one hopes so, anyway. However, I do not believe that there is as much opportunity for romance on the job among longshoremen and women, or for that matter among other blue-collar industrial workers, as there is among white-collar personnel. First of all, as of yet integration of the sexes in industry is not complete. On the waterfront and in certain other industries, men still outnumber women five, or in some places, ten to one. From that standpoint integration should have taken place sooner in blue-collar work. Women are coming into our world just as our work is disappearing, not only from automation but also from the exporting of our jobs to other countries via NAFTA and GATT. Where the opportunity to get into blue-collar work still exists, however, women are at a distinct romantic disadvantage compared to their white-collar sisters. For one thing, blue-collar women suffer from a disadvantage in dress. Work clothes are utilitarian. Hard-toe shoes, gloves, and coveralls are difficult to feminize. And I don't know what the hell a girl can do to make her hair attractive under a hard hat.

The most highly charged sexual scene I ever encountered on the job took place in Southern California. In the Port of Los Angeles, which includes San Pedro, Wilmington, and the Port of Long Beach, all longshoremen are dispatched to their jobs from one hiring hall. On the West Coast, longshoremen can take out a travel card and work in almost any other port they choose, and, about once a year, I used to choose Los Angeles for a couple of months. Fall was always nice. The weather had usually cooled off a bit by then.

In L.A. the first job out of the hiring hall I drew was long steel, landing it on deck at number two hatch on a traditional, freighter-type vessel. Number three hatch, just behind us, was loading a powdery substance in paper sacks called celite. The powder was used in water filtration systems, and Los Angeles loaded out a lot of it. It was not bad cargo. The sacks weighed fifty pounds, and you could throw them around all over the place. The gang in number three hatch was working the shelterdeck, the last deck up from the lower hold, meaning they were stowing cargo only about ten feet below the main deck.

We always draw spectators when we are working cargo. Usually, it is confined to the walking boss, the supercargo, and perhaps the vessel's second mate, checking out how we are doing the job. However, number three hatch was getting an inordinate amount of attention from the crew. There were never less than half a dozen men hanging around the hatch, looking over the coaming down to where the work was taking place. The ship was flying a flag of convenience, Liberian, I think. The officers were Greek but the crew was all Asian, Filipinos, Chinese, and perhaps two or three other nationalities. Suddenly I became aware that the number of spectators behind me had doubled. My partner and I, an L.A. longshoreman, landed our last I-beams in place, and turned the job over to the men relieving us.

"What the hell is going on back there?" I asked my partner.

"It's probably Jean. She's working that hatch," he said.

"A woman longshoreman? Haven't they ever seen a woman longshoreman before?"

"Well," he said, looking wistful and sucking in his breath, "maybe not like Jean. Come on, let's take a look."

I had to admit it—Jean did look pretty good. In Los Angeles, longshoremen are liable to wear anything when it gets hot. I have never seen bathing suits, but a lot of guys wear shorts, unless they are working barbed wire. Jean was wearing shorts, and a shapeless, floppy sweatshirt reaching down to her waist. She was a big girl, blonde, strong, of course, and her movements as she worked were absolutely graceful. And sexy! If you can conceive, that is, of sex and grace caught up in the movement of a woman grabbing a fifty-pound sack and heaving it to a pile she was building up. But Jean was like a ballet dancer; every movement she made looked good. And she was well built. When she twisted her body around, the shapeless sweatshirt would tighten and give definition to her breasts beneath the garment. Her legs were tanned, and she showed a bit of tan skin above her belt line when she stretched and threw a sack. When this happened it made the crewmen watching her catch their breath. Her gang was out from under the coaming, working in the square of the hatch. The sun was beating down on them, and they were beginning to sweat. They finished a load, and while they were waiting for the next one to come in, the girl suddenly peeled off her sweatshirt and cast it aside. She was wearing a brief tank top underneath. It was as if San Pedro had turned into Hollywood. I glanced up to the rim of the hatch. A good dozen Asian eyes rolled, and several of the observers swooned, turning away from the agony and ecstasy of it all. Jean and her partners finished another load of sacks and then turned the work over to the other half of their gang and came up on deck. She was standing right beside me, and I looked her over. She was not merely beautiful, she was stunning. All eyes were upon her, but she took it with an easy acceptance, even a smile. She was about the same size as I was, if I could have trained down to welterweight. "What?" I asked her. "What are you going to do for an encore?"

CHAPTER TEN

Race and Class

My mother never used the word "nigger." She never, for that matter, used any derogatory word to describe any member of a minority group of Americans. However, at the same time, I believe that she was inherently prejudiced against everyone who was not white. It was an egalitarian world, but a white one she came out of.

My father, on the other hand, used not only "nigger" but also every other racial term casually in use by "white" America in the early days of the twentieth century. And, purely and simply, he was not prejudiced toward anyone. He took people as they came, liked just about everyone, and appeared to be liked by everyone he met who got to know him. In his later years, when he was the shed boss much of the time, he had a coterie of Mexicans who followed him around from cantaloupe shed to cantaloupe shed, all summer long. They stuck with my father even when they could have gotten better jobs somewhere else. They stuck with him because they liked him and they liked to work for him. Significantly, the only black man I ever saw working on a packing shed was hired and put there by my father.

I have been asked by whites not connected to longshoring if, after having spent a third of a century in almost daily contact with black Americans on an equal basis, I have gained any unique insights into race and racial prejudice. I have to answer in the negative. Other than the trite observation that people are people, whatever their race, I might add that, if you are white, upon meeting a black person for the first time, you would do well to evaluate and relate to them in terms of class rather than color. That means working class in addition to middle class, and, if you are in a street environment, separating them both from the criminal class as well.

Both blacks and whites pack along a lot of racial baggage in their daily lives, whites probably more than blacks. For instance, in an election blacks find it easier to vote for a white candidate than whites do for a black candidate. The answer lies, I think, in the fact that until recently there were almost no blacks on the ballot in most of America. Black Americans had had the experience, repeatedly, of voting for white candidates because the whole slate was white. It was either vote for a white or not vote. It is breaking down somewhat now because candidates of all colors are on almost all ballots, but unless the white voter is politically involved and aware, before he puts his "X" opposite a black's name, the thought crosses his mind, will this candidate really represent all of us?

Nothing breaks down prejudices more quickly than becoming politically involved in a multiracial environment. Union politics is always a hot item on the San Francisco waterfront, and the annual elections for union offices, both the primary and the run-off, receive a lot of attention from the individual longshoremen. To say that they vote a racial ticket, which almost everyone does to some extent, is an oversimplification. I once inadvertently got an unquestionably authentic, honest, and revealing look into the union longshore vote. The resulting data opened my eyes to the mysteries of the individual voter.

Longshoremen in the Bay Area get a sample ballot in the mail about a month before the elections take place. There are over a dozen individual offices to be voted on, starting with the president and going down through the vice-president, the secretary, business agents, and a half-dozen dispatchers. In addition there are a number of committees to be filled—Executive Board, Board of Trustees, etc. This means that there may be well over a hundred candidates running for office. To expedite matters, most longshoremen mark their sample ballot at home and then take it into the voting booth with them on election day to help them get through the real ballot without relying on memory alone. After they come out of the voting booth, they drop their sample ballot in the nearest trash can.

On election eve, after the polls closed, my friend Al and I volunteered to help clean up. We each grabbed a trash can and dragged them outside to where the garbage men could pick them up. I turned to go back into the hall, but Al stood there, staring down at the trash in his can.

"What is it?" I asked.

"Here's Green's sample ballot," Al said.

"Which Green?" I asked, mildly interested. We had a lot of Greens: Cadillac Green, Toothpick Green, even Fencing Jim Green, who had almost made the Olympic team. I went back and joined Al.

"Toothpick," Al said. The sample ballot, having gone through the mail, had Green's name on it, right there staring up at us from the top of the trash. Both Al and I knew Toothpick well, having worked with him often. Al and I looked at each other, each having the same thought on our minds. Abruptly, curiosity got the better of our ethics, and we both made a grab for the sample ballot.

"Let's find out right now if that son of a bitch voted for us," Al said, unfolding the ballot. Both Al and I were running for the Executive Board, and we had campaigned together. It was our first time out, running for office.

It turned out that Toothpick Green had voted for me but not for Al, which was perplexing. Al and Toothpick were black and I was white, so race could not be the main factor. But what did Toothpick have against Al? Al grabbed up another ballot from the trash. I started going through my can. In all we collected over sixty sample ballots. Then we furtively took them off to an out-of-the-way coffee joint and spread them out in a back booth to see what they would reveal.

Out of the sample ballots Al got eight votes and I got seven, not enough, as it turned out, if projected on to the total vote, to get either of us elected to the Executive Board, but not too bad for our first time out.

Between us, Al and I could identify almost everyone whose sample ballot we had. Black voters were slanted toward black candidates and whites toward whites. Al got six black votes and I got four white. However, the most startling fact revealed by studying the ballots was that no matter how rabid a racist the voter was, and there were three or four examples present from both sides of the color line, not a single ballot we examined reflected a pure racist vote; on every identifiably racist ballot there were racial crossovers, sometimes half a dozen. Why did Toothpick Green vote for me? I'll never know. After Al and I split up that night and went home, I retrieved my sample ballot, marked up like everyone else's but discarded on the floor-board of my car. In analyzing my vote I had definite preferences for every major office, but I also cast votes through pure whim or fancy. I voted for one man, black, whom I hardly knew. We had worked to-gether once for a single day. He had been a good man to work with, and, consequently, it had been a good day. He got my vote. Probably all the other sample ballots reflected similar reasoning to some ex-tent.

Sometimes, however, race and the attitudes and problems race engenders in Americans become overwhelming to the point that you feel you would like to find another planet. White longshoremen, when no blacks were present, would occasionally mutter that "blacks are taking over the union" (and the word used was "black," not "nig-ger." The few times I heard the word "nigger" used on the water-front, it was always one black, usually drunk, addressing another black.) We had one black president who turned out to be a disaster. He made secret, handshake agreements binding on the local that were favorable to several employers, bypassed the union machinery to resolve disputes, and may even have been on the take. He was dis-credited to the point that not only was he defeated when he ran for re-election, but he had to leave town. He transferred to another port. His conduct had a negative effect on other black candidates, too. The following year a sizable number of black longshoremen did not vote, or cast blank ballots, apparently, and white candidates swept al-most all offices. A short time later I heard a white man again com-plain that blacks were taking over the union. I pointed out that the local now had a white president, a white vice-president and secre-tary, two white business agents, and most of the dispatchers were white. The only prominent office occupied by a black was that of chief business agent, held by a man universally respected by everyone. I asked the white longshoreman how, in an organization in which at least half of the membership was black, did he explain all those white officeholders?

"Gee, I never thought of that," he replied, puzzled. "How do *you* explain it?" I told him it was obviously a repudiation of black leadership by black longshoremen.

"Hmmm," he replied, but I did not see a light bulb go on over his head. A couple of years later the local officers were back in approximate racial balance again.

The most serious charge, the hardest accusation for a black to handle, is that of being an Uncle Tom—favoring white people over black—from which there is no defense. What is a black person to do to defend himself? He cannot make himself look ridiculous by appearing to keep score by pointing to the number of blacks he may have favored, or, worse still, the number of whites he has discriminated against. If, in a racially mixed company, a black charges a white with being a racist, no matter how unjust the accusation, the white cannot always expect help from other blacks in denying it, so great is the danger of being branded an "Uncle Tom." Any protest another black might raise can be construed as taking sides—the wrong side. Even if the confrontation is brought on by a black racist, ordinary, rational black men can be so intimidated that they will remain mute and cease to function. If you are a white person in a situation such as this, you may have difficulty functioning, too.

"You white honky motherfucker," Joe screamed at me. "You a white racist motherfucker!" Joe's black face was only inches away from mine. Spittle was flying from his mouth with every word he flung at me.

We were having a Board of Trustees meeting. The board, to which I had been elected only two months before, consisted of six members. The board is the financial watchdog of the union. All financial transactions pass before the trustees for review and approval. The bookkeeper was a black woman who had been on the job for about a year. The bookkeeper before her, also a black woman, had been there ten years, and she had been forced to quit over a charge for which I could never get a clear explanation, either from the secretary or from any of my fellow trustees, black or white. The only thing I knew for certain was that she was forced out of her job by a faction in the black leadership.

The new bookkeeper, a very decent and agreeable woman, was not, however, doing the job for which she had been hired. The research I had done over the two months since I had been elected to the committee had forced me to this conclusion. The bookkeeper's books were a mess. Entries were incomplete and sometimes illegible. Bank statements were irreconcilable. Cash outflow had no relationship to cash inflow. Columns of figures, which I had taken for granted to be accurate, did not even add up. I caught this one evening while doing a cursory examination of officers' and staff's salaries; the total for the month did not, somehow, seem right. It wasn't. It was off by slightly more than $1,700. It was then that I decided to take my findings to the secretary of the local and share them with him.

"Yeah, we're running out of money," the secretary said. "I guess we're going to have to ask the membership for a dues increase."

"How much?" I asked.

"I dunno. Maybe a buck or two." The secretary, a white man who had come onto the waterfront the same time as I, had got himself elected to his office for no easily discernible reason other than he had got more votes than anybody else. The news I gave him about our bookkeeper made him uneasy. I told him my guess was that the bookkeeper was honest and that there was no evidence of her stealing money. Probably she was incompetent because of a lack of training, so she might learn the job and improve over time. I also told the secretary that I would publicly support him if he asked the membership for a dues increase, but that first we had to straighten out the bookkeeping, then find out how much of an increase was needed. To do that, I suggested that he call an immediate meeting of the board of trustees and, if possible, have the outside auditor present.

"Yeah, I guess we better do that," the secretary agreed, glumly. "How about next Tuesday?"

"Fine."

"Say," he added, "why don't you talk to the auditor? You're a trustee. You can do that."

The auditor and I introduced ourselves to each other over the telephone. I identified myself as a new trustee, told him what I had discovered about the bookkeeping and the local's finances, and asked him if he would attend the trustee's meeting the coming Tuesday where we would address the problem.

"I'm not sure the secretary is aware of the seriousness of the problem," I said.

"Oh, yes, he is," the auditor responded.

"He is?"

"Yes. I laid it all out to him when he assumed office," he said, "just as I did for his predecessor last year. The union, your local, has been running a deficit for some time now. The International is concerned—we are their auditors, too. The local is in arrears to the International in its per-capita transfer. But that is just one item. There are several areas of debt. You need a dues increase."

"How much?" I asked.

"Hard to say, exactly. The books are a mess. But I would guess somewhere around five dollars a month per member." This was a bitter pill to swallow. It was going to take the willing participation of the entire leadership, all the officers, to get the rank and file to accept that kind of an increase.

"Why are the books a mess?" I asked. There was a long silence.

"Your bookkeeper," he said, finally. "She lacks education and experience in the job she was hired to do."

"Can she learn the job?" I asked.

"She has already gotten quite a bit of on-the-job training," he said.

"What do you mean?"

"We've had our people down to your office repeatedly," he replied. "Which, incidentally, is not covered by your retainer to us. If we continue to do your bookkeeper's work, we will have to bill you for our services."

"Can you attend our meeting Tuesday morning?" I asked.

"We'll send someone down there, yes."

Although I had by now been on the waterfront for fifteen years, I was taking on something new as a longshoreman. I quit working days and joined a night longshore gang so I could function as a union trustee. Nights I was blue collar. Days I began to feel like I was white collar. I even ended up with a briefcase.

The trustee's meeting Tuesday morning was well attended. The secretary's office was full to overflowing. Even the International president, Harry Bridges, was there, unquestionably to make sure any financial measures taken would include the International's getting their per-capita assessment, their only source of money to pay their staff and keep the union running up and down the coast. The man from the auditor's office looked the part: he wore glasses and had on a drab gray suit. If you were going to cast someone for a Casper Milquetoast role, he looked the part.

Most of the people present were black. In addition to a healthy sampling of ex-officers and dispatchers who were black, there were also a number of prominent black longshoremen in attendance who, while not necessarily black nationalists, nevertheless devoted most of their time and efforts to promoting black causes. I hoped that race would not enter into our proceedings and get in the way of our doing what we had to do. I was getting cold stares before the meeting even started, but I had not anticipated what was about to take place.

The secretary opened the meeting with a brief statement and then took a back seat. "It looks like we're going to need a dues increase, fellas," he said. He pointed to me. "He'll tell you all about it."

I gave a brief rundown of what I had learned by examining the ledgers and the auditor's reports. I pointed out that the situation was very serious, and that it was essential that we raise the dues enough to pay off present debts—accumulated long before the present administration came into office, I added, to get the secretary on board—and to maintain the local's financial health. I said that it would probably take a five-dollar monthly dues increase to balance the books. I added that we also had to do something about the bookkeeping; because of errors it was presently unacceptable. I nodded toward the auditor.

"Do you have anything you want to add to that?" I asked him.

"Yes," he began, "that essentially covers the deficit, but there are other items that must be addressed. There appears to have been a comingling of funds with the building association's monies, which . . ." Casper never completed his sentence. That was when

Joe leaned across the table and screamed in my face that I was a honky motherfucker. The auditor, startled, took a look at Joe, grabbed his briefcase, and fled the building.

There was no interrupting Joe. He was rabid and hysterical. I looked around for some kind of rescue, looked to the rational, composed black men present, whom I had brought up to date on our financial and bookkeeping situation before the meeting. They remained silent and avoided my eyes.

"You're a motherfucker," Joe repeated in a scream. "You're a honky white racist motherfucker. You don't like the bookkeeper because she's black."

"What's black got to do with it?" I demanded, shouting back at him. There was a knock on the door. For some reason this silenced Joe. There was another rapping, and then the door opened and the woman under discussion entered the room. She had a sheaf of papers in her hand. The poor woman was obviously frightened. She dropped the papers in front of the secretary and quickly left, closing the door behind her.

"I had the bookkeeper prepare a financial statement for this meeting," the secretary said, distributing the papers around the table. "This will tell you where we are."

Everyone took a silent recess to read, or pretend to read, the financial report. I was startled to discover that the report was essentially a copy of an earlier financial summation, the one where the officer's salaries did not add up. I decided to remain silent, hoping someone else would bring up the error.

"Well, there ain't no honkey motherfucker going to fire nobody because they're black," Joe announced loudly. Several of his colleagues nodded their head and voiced agreement.

"Well, she is not doing an acceptable job," I said.

"You saying she can't do the job because she's black," Joe exploded.

"What's black got to do with it?" I countered. "We had a black bookkeeper before this woman . . . Betty. She was good. She was competent. I've been over her books. She was very good."

"You're a white motherfucker," Joe repeated doggedly. His friends behind him muttered assent.

"Look," I said, picking up the bookkeeper's report. "Maybe in time this woman can be trained to do the job. I don't know. But right now she is winging it. If the auditors hadn't warned us, we wouldn't even know what shape we're in. We don't even know for sure how much money we've got in the bank. Here." I held the report up in front of Joe and his friends. "Add up this column of figures. They don't even make sense." Nobody said anything. I turned to the secretary.

"You have a calculator there. You add them up," I demanded.

The secretary dutifully added up the column. He knew what the figures would reveal. He tore off the tape, glanced at it, and passed it around the table.

"See, her figures don't even add up," I said.

"You a honky motherfucker."

I picked up the latest auditor's report and held it up before Joe and his crew. "Well, this honky motherfucker is telling you that we are out of money," I said. "And as trustees and members of this union it is up to us to do something about it. We cannot ignore it." This set off another torrent of racial abuse. No one present seemed to be able to want to attempt to stem it. Finally, Bridges spoke.

"Anyone could 'ave been a racist," he said. "But people can

change. People change." I did not know what the hell that was supposed to mean, but it seemed to break the spell. Everyone stirred in his chair.

Andy, black, and a friend, spoke up. "How much of an increase in dues do you figure we need?" he asked the secretary. The secretary pursed his lips and appeared to give the question some serious thought.

"I figure we could get by with a couple of dollars more a month," the secretary said. Andy turned to me.

"How much do you think we need?" he asked.

"At least twice that. Even if we lay off one of the business agents," I said. I waited for the secretary to contest my statement, but he remained silent. He was probably winging it, too.

"Mothah Fuckah," someone directed at me. The tone had changed. It was not a shout. Someone was just winding down.

Bridges rose. "Well, you guys are going to 'ave to get together and solve this problem," he said, making for the door to escape back uptown to the International offices. "Yer going to 'ave to level with the membership. Yer going to 'ave to ask for a dues increase . . . unless you want the International Executive Board to throw your local into receivership and send someone down here to run things for you."

I had to admire Harry Bridges. Without appearing to offer a solution, he had indicated what the local had to do, and he had issued an ultimatum and a threat. Receivership would throw all those present who were holding down paid jobs out of their warm offices and put them back to working cargo on the waterfront again. After Bridges left, it remained quiet in the room.

"Now, about this auditor's report," I said, breaking the silence. I did not hear anymore "motherfuckers" thrown at me for the rest of the meeting.

Racial prejudice, which is irrational, can usually be erased in an individual by education and close contact with peoples of other colors. Class, however, is another matter. Class indoctrination begins at birth and once imbued in a person seems to accompany him or her to death. Some people, despite complete failures of character, still feel they are intrinsically better than others, and many of those others carry a feeling of inferiority with them to their grave. Being born in America can enable one to escape much of this, but class in the United States still exists. Moreover, it can be even more complicated than in other societies, with results both good and bad since, unlike the rest of the world, class in America is interpreted in not one, but two ways.

The classic separation of people into aristocrats, the bourgeoisie, and peasants is still strong in many Third World countries. Remnants of this stratification of their citizens may also be encountered on occasion in such odd corners of the earth as England, France, Italy, and other parts of darkest Europe.

Americans, although no less susceptible than anyone else to inner feelings of superiority for various other reasons, are invariably startled when they encounter the phenomenon of class structure while stumbling around in someone else's country. A number of years ago while riding horseback deep in rural Mexico, a companion and I came upon a boy astride a burro coming down a trail toward us herding four cows. The upper slope of the hillside was fenced pasture. Four strands of barbed wire protected it from entry. The downslope was rough, open range. We drew our horses aside to let the boy, perhaps ten years of age, drive his small herd past us. Just then down the hill toward the fence came a jenny, a female burro. Ears up and alert, she stopped a few yards beyond the fence opposite us, swishing her tail.

The jack burro the boy was riding suddenly came to life. He rolled his eyes, snorted, and then reared and threw the boy off. Riderless, the jack headed straight for the jenny, on the other side of the fence, which, I assume, was in heat.

The jack's ardor was such that he did not concede an obstacle between them. He hit the fence so hard it made a loud wrenching sound. The barbed wire stretched, held, and then propelled the donkey back. The beast, undeterred, gathered himself and lunged at the fence again. On the third try a wire snapped and the burro fought his way through the fence to the other side. The jack's first shot at the fence had so alarmed the jenny that she took off on a dead run away from him. Once free of the barbed wire, the jack gave chase. The last we saw of them the jenny was disappearing over the hill with the jack hot on her tail.

My companion and I dismounted. I handed my reins to her and helped the boy to his feet. He was rubbing his butt where he had hit the ground, but he did not appear to be severely injured. He was, however, alarmed and frightened. As he stood there gazing off to where the two animals had disappeared, his lower lip quivered. I thought he might be about to cry.

"Oh . . . oh . . . oh," he wailed. "Quiero miedo que mi padre . . . furioso . . . Tengo miedo." He was frightened of what his father might do to him over the loss of his burro. The four cows had stopped and were turned toward us. They were staring at us as if awaiting instructions. Apparently they did not have plans to go anywhere.

"Oh . . . oh . . . oh," the boy wailed. A tear rolled down and dropped off one cheek. There was a gate to the enclosed pasture a short distance down in the direction from which my companion and I had come.

"No tienes miedo," I said to him. I indicated the gate. "Hay un puerto alla." I took my reins back and placed them in his hands.

"Tenga el caballo. Vaya! Go get your burro."

The boy's mouth dropped open. The look of fear left his face and was replaced by one of wonderment. "El caballo?" he said incredulously, staring at the horse.

"Si. Tengalo. Vaya! Pronto, pronto!" If he waited too long, he would never catch up with his jackass.

"Oh, no, gracias, Señor. Gracias, pero no. Un caballo? Para mi a montar? Gracias, no." He shook his head emphatically. It was my turn to be incredulous. With my limited Spanish I tried to force my mount on him, but he would not accept it. The idea of his usurping a señor's horse was unthinkable. As great as were the fears of the consequences of the burro getting away from him and possibly lost, and unquestionably severely lacerated by the barbed wire, they could not override his sense of conduct and what was proper to him in his social class. Already implanted at the age of ten.

Class-consciousness of this kind simply does not exist in America. But class of another kind does, and all Americans understand and acknowledge it, whatever their social position or color. Everyone without exception hopes his or her conduct does not indicate a lack of it, a lack of class. To say someone has class is the highest compliment one American can pay to another. And the word is class, not classy. Classy conveys a sense of style and manner, which can be acquired, or even faked. Class is something one possesses, something innate. Being innate, class is also intangible and therefore easier to describe than define.

I once got into a fight with a black longshoreman at an Executive Board meeting of our union. It was not much of a fight, and it was broken up before either of us could do much damage to the other. It

happened essentially because I lost control. Not that I wasn't pro-
voked. The man, whose name was Stitch, was loud and abusive, and
everything he said and did was designed to call attention to himself.
His conduct was generally dismissed by everyone around the hiring
hall and at work, but on this occasion he had invaded the Executive
Board meeting and disrupted it to the point where nothing was getting done. Stitch was looking for a confrontation and found one in
the person of me; I made a motion to evict him. He seconded my
motion by challenging me to do it. In the resulting scuffle, I threw
three punches, only one of which connected and only lightly. The
final result was the fight was broken up, the meeting was adjourned,
and nothing at all was accomplished.

The reaction of the longshoremen I worked with was carefully
limited. In the hiring hall the following morning, a couple of white
longshoremen expressed regret that I had not "kicked the shit out of
him." I remained silent about that; perhaps it did not occur to them
that, if the fight had continued on, he might have kicked the shit out
of *me*. My black friends carefully avoided the subject, but, in a typical
black manner of showing friendship and support, would come up,
say hello, and stand beside me for a few moments. The definitive
statement on the matter, nevertheless, was made two days later by a
black man.

Bob was a younger longshoreman who had been promoted pre-
maturely to walking boss on merit. I knew Bob well. Before his promotion we had worked together on numerous occasions. He was an
excellent walking boss. He had the ability, not at all common among
bosses, of making you feel that you were working with him, instead
of for him. Two days after the incident at the Executive Board meeting, I got a forklift job at the pier where Bob was working. After I entered the gate, I got my lift, drove it down, and parked by the ship,

waiting for someone to give me an assignment. A few moments later Bob drove up in a company pick-up truck and stopped next to my lift. We were face to face, only a few feet separating us. Bob looked at me and shook his head.

"What the hell's wrong with you, anyway?'

"Why? What do you mean?"

"I heard you got into a fight with that Stitch at an Executive Board meeting," Bob said.

"Oh, that. It wasn't much of a fight," I said.

"Well," Bob said, shaking his head again, as if he were having difficulty believing what he had heard, "what the hell are you doing responding to a no-class asshole like that?" He put the pick-up in gear.

"How about helping me out on number five hatch?" he said as he drove away.

CHAPTER ELEVEN

The Violent Men

Vic was a kidder. We have all known the type. Vic never came up to you and said, "Hello, how are you?" He introduced himself with a dig, usually insulting. "Hey, Champ, you still chasing ratty-ass pussy?" was one of his more charming examples. Of course, like most of his ilk, he could dish it out, but he could not take it.

Vic also was going bald, and it bothered him. Vic was about forty-five, which is as good a time as any, I guess, if you are going to go bald, but Vic went for a hair transplant.

Using some kind of an instrument, the doctor took little plugs of follicles out of the back of Vic's skull, where he had a lot of hair, and plunged them into his forehead, where he had none. At first Vic faced us each day with rows of tiny scabs, which itched ferociously. Eventually the scabs developed into little wisps of hair. Through it all, Vic remained the same old Vic. When my former wife and I were going through a divorce, Vic was always good for something like, "So she finally threw your ass out, huh, Sport?"

"Go away, Vic. Go somewhere else."

The routine never grew old with Vic, but eventually it precipitated a crisis. Waiting for the dispatch to begin one day, three or four others and I were standing around talking about nothing in particular when Vic came up to our group. His implanted hair had grown out to a sparse and straggly couple of inches. It stood straight up. Vic was afraid to comb it, afraid that he might pull some of it out.

"Man," he said to me. "I saw your new girl friend, and, man, is she ugly!"

"You better not let her hear you say that," I said. "She'll kick your ass!"

"No, I mean it. I saw her, and she . . . is . . . ugly!"

"Yeah?" I responded. "Well, at least she isn't going with a guy whose forehead looks like an armpit."

It just popped out of me. I must have read it somewhere; it was the funniest thing I said all week. It got hee-haws from everybody. Hell, even I was laughing. Vic, however, was livid. He wanted to fight. He came at me throwing punches.

"Help!" I yelled, retreating. "Help! Scotty? Pruitt? Help! Pull him off of me!" I got behind Brooks, who had a lot of bulk. Every time Vic tried to dodge around him, Brooks, laughing, would throw a block on him. Then the dispatch started, and Vic had to get in line to get his job.

Shortly afterward Vic transferred over to the ship's clerks, and I did not see him for a while. I finally ran into him one day about a year later. He had forgotten all about our fracas. He had a pretty good head of hair. It did not look at all bad.

This is the level at which violence occurs on the West Coast waterfronts. It is almost always personal and usually takes place with a minimum of physical damage to the participants. Unlike in the movies, it is never lethal.

In the movies, waterfronts are sinister places that exist only at night during a light rain where car chases take place over wet streets illuminated by headlights and punctuated by gunshots, screeching tires, and breaking glass. Very rarely do you see any work getting done on the piers down there.

I would not argue that we do not have violent men working the docks. We have more than our share of psychopaths and sociopaths calling themselves longshoremen. But other than someone throwing an occasional punch or two, our workplace is free of violence. All the psychopaths seem to practice their criminal activity off the waterfront. There are penalties against assault on the job, of course, written into our labor contract, but just like the statutes in the criminal code, the law does not always eliminate the deed. The principal deterrent is an unspoken understanding among us all that the problems and issues that arise on the waterfront are too important to be settled by practicing violence on each other.

In the past, violence was endemic to the waterfronts of West Coast America. It is possible, I suppose, that it could become so again. The maritime strikes in the thirties and those shortly after World War II were bitterly fought wars—longshoremen and seamen versus shipping and stevedoring interests who used police, National Guardsmen, and hired goons against the strikers. The longshoremen responded with muscle of their own. But there was a difference: nowhere on the West Coast did the longshoremen use professional goons. The strikers were workers first, longshoremen, and when the strike was over, they went back to work and their muscle squads ceased to exist. The company goons went off somewhere else to hire themselves out to management in another strike.

Whenever possible the union tried to make serving on the anti-scab squads compulsory for everyone. Everybody was supposed to take part. Some people can engage in violence willingly, some even enthusiastically, others less so. The last strike in which the waterfront employers attempted to use scabs was a few years after World War II. Asher, an older longshoreman I knew, once told my partner and me of his tour of duty on one of those committees.

They worked in threes: Asher, Willie, and Tony. Before they gave a scab a beating, they gave him a chance to mend his ways. If he was scabbing because he was hungry, they offered to take care of him, give him a chit, and send him down to the Strike Committee, which would feed him and his family. If he was married, and he rejected their appeal, they would pay a friendly visit to his home first before they worked him over.

Asher, soft spoken and educated, was not what one would call a pugnacious person. Together with Willie, an enormous black man, the two would come to the man's house about dinner time. Tony came into the action later, if needed.

The dinner hour was good because the man was likely to be surrounded by his wife and family. With Willie standing off to one side, Asher, innocuous in appearance and not constituting any great threat, would knock on the front door. If someone inside demanded to know who it was, Asher would hold up an envelope and sing out, "Telegram . . . Western Union." The instant the door was opened, even if only a slight crack, Willie would shove on through. Followed by Asher, Willie would confront the man, usually seated at the kitchen table. Asher would then make a short speech to the effect that the man was working during a trade-union dispute—taking their jobs, so to speak—and if he continued to do so, it would go very hard on him. That was Asher's role. All Willie had to do was tower over everybody and look ugly. Willie was chosen for his role because many of the scabs were white men from the South, and the sight of a big, muscular black man in an assertive posture was unquestionably unnerving. Upon finishing his little speech, Asher and Willie would abruptly turn and stalk out, usually leaving the wife in hysterics. Tony was waiting in the car with the motor running for a fast getaway in case someone alerted the police. It was a tactic that worked very well on most scabs, but then the trio ran up against a professional strikebreaker. He continued working despite every warning. They had to back up their threat.

Tony's weapon of preference was the steel head off of a rather large ball-peen hammer. Grasped firmly in the palm of his right fist, it was a considerable article of influence. In addition, Tony was a Sunday artist, meaning one of his Sunday punches coming out of nowhere was usually enough to lay a man out. The man who was to be the target of their punishment took a bus to work, and he got off at the pier head where the cops were waiting to escort him inside— no chance of getting him there. The trio decided to take him when he left home. They had him staked out. Willie and Asher were in a doorway out of sight. When the scab ran to get on the bus, Tony was just getting off. The scab never knew what hit him. Willie and Asher came out of their hiding place in the doorway, and the three of them grabbed the man, who was down prone on the sidewalk. The plan was to drag the scab over to the gutter, lay his legs across the curb, and jump up and down on them until one of them broke.

"That's when everything came apart," Asher said. Asher was relating the story to my partner Montgomery and me. We three were sitting in this coffee joint, looking out at the Bay, waiting for the ship to come in. It was about ten-thirty in the morning. The ship was late. We had been waiting since eight o'clock, on the payroll collecting all that gravy. Both Montgomery and I were suckers for old-timers. We could listen to them by the hour.

"What happened?" my partner demanded.

"Yeah, what the hell happened?" I echoed Montgomery.

"Well, there was this woman . . . got off the bus right behind Tony. She started screaming bloody murder. I had one of the guy's legs, Tony had the other, and Willie had him by the arms. We were dragging him over to the curb, but the woman was raising so much hell, I had to do something. I dropped my leg and rushed over to her.

'This is a bona fide, legally sanctioned, trade-union dispute,' I told her. 'You'd best be on your way.' She kept on screaming. A couple of people across the street were staring at us. It looked as if a crowd might gather. I took the woman by the arm and attempted to lead her away. I didn't know what the hell to do.

'This is a legally sanctioned, bona fide trade-union dispute,' I started to say again, and then I heard this WHOMP! and Tony started screaming.

'OOOOH!' Tony yelled, clutching his crotch. The scab had come to, and, using his free leg, the one I'd let go of, kicked Tony in the balls. Tony was bent over, groaning. I rushed over to them. The scab was struggling, thrashing around. Willie was holding him down. Suddenly, Tony straightened up.

'You son of a bitch!' Tony screamed at the scab. 'I'll kill you.' Tony jumped on top of the man. He still had the ball-peen hammerhead in his hand, and he started clubbing the guy with it. 'I'll kill you. You son of a bitch, I'll kill you!' "

"It was a real mess," Asher said, shaking his head. "Tony really was trying to kill the guy. I grabbed Tony's arm, but I was no match for him. He was a maniac. I yelled at Willie to help me. Willie dropped the man's arms and grabbed hold of Tony. Between the two of us, we managed to pull Tony off the scab. Tony was still struggling, we were holding him down, when suddenly the scab jumped up and ran off down the street. The last we saw of him he was running kitty-corner across a park down at the end of the block. Tony quit struggling, finally, so we let him up.

'Let's get the hell out of here,' Willie said, and took off up an alley. Tony was all doubled up in pain, groaning. I had to help him walk. We had to go around the corner and then about a block and a half up the street to where his car was parked. We never even got to the corner before the cops picked us up."

"How'd it go with the police? Did the cops take it out on you?"

"Yeah, did the cops work you over?"

"The cops treated us okay," Asher replied. "They didn't even book us, and they let us go that afternoon. Those cops, they had come a long way since the strikes back in the thirties. They took us to North Station and put us in a holding cell. We were in there all day, and then this captain comes in. He sits down and pulls out this card.

'See this?' he says. 'This is my withdrawal card from the Iron Workers Union. Yeah, I'm a union man, too. But I'm also a cop. Now, listen, you two. If you had grabbed that scab just two blocks west of where we picked you up, you would have been out of my jurisdiction. Remember that next time!' "

Asher grinned at us. "Then he turned us loose."

CHAPTER TWELVE

Gabfest

Although automation, through the elimination of jobs, has cut into the social aspects of blue-collar work—there just aren't as many people left around to talk to anymore—one of the rewards of doing physical labor for a living is that it gives you plenty of time to think. A job on an assembly line may be boring because of its demand to repeat the same task over and over again, but once you learn the job, your mind is relatively free even if your hands are occupied. This is simply not true of those who make their livings giving their constant attention to a computer.

In those blue-collar work situations where workers still come together to perform a common job, however, talk goes on constantly, and the conversation can cover just about every topic imaginable. This ability of blue-collar workers to socialize may have been a contributing facter in the original success of trade unions in gaining their allegiance. The workers had ample time on the job to come to conclusions about their work and get themselves organized, which is the precursor to any kind of action.

If socializing on the job leads to solidarity, longshoremen, who have traditionally worked in gangs, have a leg up on everybody else. Indeed, I know of no longshoremen throughout the world, banded together in trade unions or not, who are not strongly organized to protect themselves and their interests. San Francisco is not an exception. I can remember any number of burning arguments and discussions taking place down in the hold of a ship concerning our work and our working conditions. Many of these issues were carried over and brought up at the next union meeting.

Frequently the talk was prompted by the cargo and had nothing to do with us, with politics, or even longshoring. Once, while discharging apples from the hold of an Australian ship, one of the guys in the gang flipped a box up on its end so he could better read the label.

"Hey," he said to no one in particular, "where the hell's Tasmania?"

"It's an island off the southern coast of Australia," I answered. "Why?"

"It's where these apples come from," he replied. Everyone took note of what was a somewhat interesting fact, and then the talk died down while we made up our loads to be discharged. But the discussion was not over. One man stopped work, turned, and directed a question at me.

"Well, who the hell lives there?" he asked. I did not reply immediately, uncertain of whether or not the people of that island identified themselves first as Australians, or Tasmen. I did not have to answer. It was answered for me.

"Tasmanians, asshole," someone said. "Who do you think lives there? Hindus?"

This resulted in a round of jeers, oaths, yaks, and finally the comment that it takes one asshole to recognize another one. This had about died down when an additional question was raised.

"What color are they?"

We were a racially mixed gang. Questions involving color were usually—not always, but usually—taken seriously. Everyone mulled the question over in silence.

"They are white," I answered finally.

"All of them?"

I was stumped. I could not answer the question. "I don't know," I said. "I don't know if there are any indigenous Tasmanians living there or not. What do you think, George?" I threw the question to someone else to answer.

George was a circumspect man, slightly older than the rest of us. George had fought in the Spanish Civil War in the Abraham Lincoln Battalion of the International Brigade. When the Spanish Republic fell to the Franco forces, George escaped to France, came home, and then spent World War II in the Army fighting Japanese in the Pacific. George was one of perhaps two dozen veterans of the war in Spain who ended up working on the San Francisco waterfront. The Spanish War veterans occupied an exalted position of respect among other longshoremen who were politically left-wing. After a few years on the waterfront, I had met most of them, and after every introduction the appendage was added that so-and-so "fought in Spain, you know." These veterans took it gracefully, even modestly, but I think that over time most of them found it a little tiresome. I found it curious. I had known heroes, but I had never known icons. Years later George and I became close, but when I first met him I decided to shake him up a little bit, just to check him out. After the initial handshake and "George fought in Spain, you know," I kept a solid grip on his right hand.

"Oh, yeah?" I said. "Which side?"

Everyone else gasped, but George smiled affably. "The losing side, of course," he replied.

Down in the hold that day Tasmania was still being discussed when lunch time came. While making our way to the ladder, George asked me to cover for him when we went back to work, saying that he might be a little late. George was late, but not enough to make a difference. After we got our first few loads built and sent out, he pulled out a sheet of lined notebook paper.

"The last full-blooded Tasmanian," he announced, reading from the paper, "died in 1892. The last person with Tasmanian blood—it didn't say how much—died in 1916. Tasmanian natives were essentially the same as the Australian aborigines." George had gone home during lunch hour and consulted his encyclopedia.

"Hey," he said in wonderment, almost as an afterthought, "did you guys know that Australian natives are born *blonde!* That they stay that way until they reach the age of twelve or thirteen?" Yeah, George, thanks, now we're going to talk about hair all afternoon.

George entered union politics and eventually went on to be elected secretary-treasurer of our local. George was scrupulously honest and made one of the best secretaries we ever had. I was vice-president once when he was secretary, and we worked well together. George rarely discussed politics in ideological terms—a trait I found present in many ex-communists—but he would talk about anything if I brought it up. He knew where I stood. I once told him that I thought one of the failures of Marxists was their inability to apply their own system of analysis to themselves. That they felt that their doctrine placed them above History, outside of History, that they *were* History. I said that this intellectual elitism was not only an unhealthy conceit, but that it was anti-Marxist. I added that, without this critical restraint, Marxism on its own authority led the Soviet Union down through the years to Stalin, Stalinism, and the Gulag, and that it took a big hunk of the European and American Left with it. I summed it up by saying that the failure of the Left to achieve democratic socialism in the twentieth century lies at the door of Stalinism. Stalinism discredited Socialism.

I thought that my indictment would surely be enough to needle George into a response, but I was wrong. He gave my speech a moment of consideration before replying. "Yeah, I guess you're probably right," he said.

George died a few years ago of asbestosis. We used to work asbestos a lot in our port. In the early days we unloaded bales of it from South Africa. Then later we loaded tons upon tons of it aboard ships for export. They mined it up in the Sierra foothills in the Mother Lode country where gold was discovered.

CHAPTER THIRTEEN

The Making of a Rust Belt

A painful work loss with endless ramifications occurs when an industry shuts down a factory and moves the whole operation overseas. Everything, the jobs, the bustle of the work scene, all the life the factory supported very quickly vanish.

Automation began to have a serious impact on our waterfront work toward the end of the 1970s. The cargo containers had been in place for a decade, but their introduction had been gradual and their effect softened by attrition. Retiring workers were not replaced, so there was an ongoing decrease in longshoremen to share the decreasing work. Then suddenly, there just wasn't very much work at all. Everything was being stowed in oceangoing containers. A dozen men were doing the work of a hundred. We longshoremen had the fail-safe contractual guarantee of a weekly wage if the work fell off due to automation, meaning, if we lost the work, we did not lose the whole paycheck. However, the ease and economy of overseas shipments started having a tremendous impact on other workers, workers in industries where they could not protect themselves. In the past many of these workers had come to us in time of need, and we had helped them out. Now, even though we were up against the wall ourselves, they still came.

Over the years when we had surplus work on the waterfront, we spread it around. The unemployed from our sister locals within the ILWU and other blue-collar workers who were on strike got first priority. On big days when there was extra work, they could come down to the waterfront and earn some much needed money. The longshoremen regarded it as a natural extension of working-class solidarity. On really big days when the port was jammed with ships, we extended this work opportunity to everyone, white-collar workers included. Once when the car salesmen on Auto Row went out on strike, we gave them jobs. And then there were the cops. The first time I saw policemen show up, I was new to the waterfront and it was startling.

"Hey? What the hell is going on?" I wanted to know. "Why are we putting cops to work?" I was immediately silenced.

"Take it easy, fella," an old-timer quickly cautioned me. We were standing out on the pier head waiting to turn-to when these four guys showed up on their day off with job tickets. Two of them were even wearing their cop's shirts, with those little grommets built into the pockets so their badges could be attached without tearing up the fabric.

"I don't get it," I said.

"Don't be dumb," the old-timer said. "The next time we go out on strike, we want these guys on our side."

Eventually, automation hit us so hard, we did not have enough work for ourselves, much less jobs to give away. It was then that things got particularly grim. Workers, delegates from other industries, began showing up at our executive board meetings asking for help. Even if we had no work to give them, perhaps we had some ideas, advice as to what they could do for themselves. One typical group was composed of six men from a factory that made diesel-driven pumps and turbines whose entire blue-collar workforce was being phased out, many laid off with only two weeks notice. The oldest, a man of about sixty, had thirty-eight years on the job. He was in slightly better shape than the others; in addition to Social Security, he was to become eligible for a small industry pension in a few years when he reached sixty-five. Their story was unique in that their jobs were being eliminated by an act of legislation.

When the State of California put together the Central Valley Project, a very large system of dams and canals designed to trap and save water (the runoff from the Sierra's winter snow pack) and pump it to the arid parts of the state where it was desperately needed, a rider was tacked onto the legislative bill requiring all equipment used by the project to be American-made. It was a typical move, one of many designed to generate American jobs and support American industry. This measure fostered the creation of a medium-sized factory in which these men built diesel-driven pumps and other related items. The workforce of 400 employees had a large contingent of engineering and technical personnel. These people designed the equipment, and the blue-collar people built it. The system, which used the product of their efforts, stretched almost a thousand miles up and down the state of California.

For over forty years the factory prospered and expanded. It had come out of World War II with a practically nonexistent workload, so the Central Valley Project unquestionably gave it new life. The

International Association of Machinists (IAM), the trade union representing the blue-collar workforce, negotiated labor contracts over the years approximately the equal of the nationwide standard, and as America prospered, so did this factory and the workers along with it. Until, that is, an administration in the state capitol not friendly to labor eliminated the domestic-products clause in the original bill.

Almost immediately the equilibrium of the factory changed. Equipment that was becoming obsolete was not scheduled for replacement, and some of the newer machinery was packaged up and sent to South Korea. The handwriting was on the wall. The IAM, taking an overall strategic position, attempted to get the white-collar and engineering personnel to join in a common effort to save the plant and, consequently, everyone's job. The overture was not so much rejected as it was let die. It was simply not acted upon. The engineering faction, the most highly skilled of the white-collar force, did not feel themselves threatened. Their jobs appeared secure, and they felt their careers would always be intact. If the blue-collar workforce was to compete in what was becoming a world economy, the factory executives maintained publicly, they would have to make themselves more efficient, more competitive, and, if necessary, perhaps give up some of their fringe benefits, maybe even forego a wage increase. Management was pushing for more economic concessions from labor even as they were making plans to move their entire operation overseas.

Within a six-month period, the blue-collar workforce had been devastated by layoffs until there were not very many of them left. Of those who remained, six of them were appearing before our executive board. The president of the local was presiding. After they laid out their problem, everyone remained silent.

"Well," the president finally said, "has anyone got any ideas?" All the local's officers were present, including the chief dispatcher.

"Have we got any extra work coming up?" someone asked.

"There won't be enough work tomorrow morning," the chief dispatcher answered, "to dispatch half the available longshoremen. It's going to be the same all the way through next week. And I don't see much improvement after that." Everyone mulled that over for a while.

"Why don't we shut them down?" one of the business agents asked, his voice rising in anger.

"How?" the president asked.

The business agent turned to the group of six. "All that machinery comes in from Korea in containers now. Right?" The six men conferred in whispers for about a minute.

"Yes," said the older man, who appeared to be their spokesman. The other five nodded their heads vigorously. Hey, these were longshoremen! This finally sounded like action!

"Okay," the business agent said. "Put up a picket line. If you put up a picket line, we don't have to cross it. We won't unload those containers." The six machinists looked confused.

"How the hell are they going to do that?" asked the president. "Are they going to picket the whole damn waterfront?"

"Yeah," someone chimed in. "For the picket line to be legitimate—not get a restraining order slapped on our ass—the picket line has to be around their place of work."

"Okay," the business agent responded. "Here's what they do. They throw up a picket line around their plant. Then they extend it down to the waterfront. They can do that. It's an extended picket line because that's their work inside those containers. It doesn't violate the secondary boycott provisions of the Taft-Hartley law, either—there's been a legal ruling on that." The business agent turned to the six.

"You guys still unload the stuff from Korea, don't you?" The six went into a whispered conference again.

"You still haven't told us what piers they're going to picket," the president said to the business agent.

"The pier where the containers with the stuff from Korea are being discharged," the B.A. replied.

"Goddamn it," the president shot back, "there's a lot of containers coming in from Korea. Even the ship's clerks don't know what's in half of them." Arguments broke out among several members of the Executive Board.

The leader of the delegation cleared his throat. Everyone shut up and looked at him in expectation. Neither he nor his companions appeared too happy.

"Um," he said glumly. "Um . . . we still do some work out on the loading dock. Sorting, mostly. But most of the containers go directly to various sites up and down the state." He brightened a bit. "We do know where most of these locations are, however."

The problems manifesting themselves for the workers at that pump and turbine factory were not going to be solved by picket lines, or even goon squads. Whatever help they expected from us longshoremen was not forthcoming. We could not do anything for them, except take up a collection of money to give them at the next union meeting.

The fate of the factory was that it very shortly ceased to exist. The engineers and other white-collar people made a mistake in not joining their blue-collar brothers in an attempt to save their pump works. If they had gotten together early enough, they might have had some success. As it turned out, most of their jobs disappeared, too. A short time later the company farmed out everything but the intricate design work to subcontractors. The factory is still there, however. The windows that aren't boarded up are broken, and the railroad siding has weeds growing up between the ties.

CHAPTER FOURTEEN

Semiskilled Need Not Apply

It is a truth universally acknowledged in America that an unskilled worker who finds himself out of work has only himself to blame. He or she should have been skilled.

The contention that a modern industrial state needs a continuous and ongoing supply of skilled and educated workers may be a truism, but that does not exempt it from examination. America needs all kinds of workers, skilled and unskilled, to do the work that America needs to get done. Meaning, brain surgeons are important, but do not leave out the garbage collectors. That America is failing to produce workers in any given category remains to be proven. If Silicon Valley firms' complaints are valid—that they cannot get native workers of a certain skill—one would expect their complaint to call for an overhaul of America's education and training programs where they are failing. Instead, they indict themselves and their own hiring practices by pressuring Congress to raise immigration quotas so that they can place foreigners in these jobs. Curiously, these immigrants imported to fill skilled jobs in a modern industrial state are coming mostly from places like India, Southeast Asia, the Middle East, essentially Third World countries not widely celebrated for exemplary educational facilities.

Every time it is proposed to expand the immigration quotas to import workers for the computer industries, local newspapers in these areas are deluged with letters from Americans who are educated in computer sciences, many with advanced degrees, who could not get an interview much less a job. Their common conclusion is that there are skilled workers available, but Silicon Valley's executives want people who will work cheap. Immigrant aliens routinely receive only one-half to two-thirds the pay that Americans get and, as immigrants, are locked into their jobs as a condition of employment. It is a curious situation. We contribute to unemployment among our people by exporting their jobs, and to further unemployment among them by importing aliens to take their place in other domestic jobs they might fill. In other words, we are exporting jobs and importing workers. This does not describe a mercantile system that makes a great deal of sense.

There are people in our country, however, who argue to the contrary. One of America's most prestigious institutes, a Washington D.C. think tank making as its task the study of world trade, whose members and advocates include the top leadership of both the Republican and Democratic parties—including the immediate past president—insists that for every job exported, American citizens collectively garner anywhere between $100,000 and $1,000,000 in savings, with the average pegged at $170,000. Their reasoning is that it "costs" this much money to "save" one American's job instead of exporting his work to another country. The article of manufacture, whatever it is, will then be imported back here and sold to us more cheaply. By their twisted reasoning, the resulting savings to American consumers will be six times the cost of retraining or relocating that worker or, if he remains unemployed, supporting him or her on welfare. Carrying this reasoning a bit further, perhaps we Americans should begin an immediate sales campaign to vend all our jobs on the foreign market. Of course we will all end up on welfare, but think of all the money to be made. And we should begin without any undue delay; automation is an ongoing threat, and every loss of a job in that direction reduces by one our export product. Which jobs should we sell first? Our export program, of course, must be put together with an eye toward conforming to the provisions of NAFTA and the World Trade Organization, the successor to GATT. But I would propose that among our first offerings we include the jobs being held down by those people working in a certain think tank in Washington D.C.

Can one assign a price to someone's existence? Can one assign a dollar amount to a family's, a community's, or a region's economic and cultural loss when work goes? It was not just the working class that suffered when vast areas of the Midwest were turned into a rust belt. Except for the very wealthy, who can construct their milieu wherever they choose, unknown numbers of lives were severely damaged and disrupted among blue-collar and white-collar classes alike. No one can know the true costs, other than in money, to those in the Rust Belt other than the people who lived there and survived it.

Make-work programs, jobs that are created for no other reason than to keep someone busy, are constantly under attack, and I for one look forward to their complete elimination. Presently in America, work and the concept of jobs seem to have lost their definitions. Work is an activity, whether blue collar or white collar, in which one engages to produce something valuable and needed in the world. A job is something one holds down to perform work. Fostering jobs in the world is a noble endeavor. Making work can be a sin.

There used to be a walking boss on our waterfront whom everyone avoided working for. On a container ship there is a vital piece of equipment called a locking-cone that is used when containers are stacked on deck, one on top of the other. After the first, and each succeeding layer, of containers is loaded aboard, men are lifted up by the crane on top of them to place one of these cones in receptacles at the four corners of each van and then lowered down again. The crane driver then brings in the next layer of vans and places each one exactly on top of the container below, nesting all four corners into the cones, which are then locked, securing that layer of vans to the one below it. This operation is repeated until the last, the sixth, layer of vans is aboard. Then the whole block of vans is secured to the ship's deck with long steel rods and turn-buckles.

The work is not easy. The turn-buckles are heavy, the steel rods are heavy, and even the cones are not light—some of them, depending on the equipment used, weigh thirty pounds, although in dirty weather you never carry more than two of them across the top of the exposed vans. The pace of the work is very fast. When the men are up on top, the crane is idle, so there is an effort on everyone's part to get the crane back to lifting vans again as soon as possible. The lashing crew may get a break between layers of vans, but there is also a lot of other work to be done; rods and turn-buckles must be got ready and cones have to be sorted out.

When working for this one walking boss, there always seemed to be something pressing that had to be done, something calling for our immediate attention. We never seemed to get a break. We may have been busting our asses lashing down a block of vans and finally got what we thought was going to be a respite so we could fall out and regain our strength for the next go-round, when Chuck would show up.

"Hey, guys, we're going to need some more cones for number nine hatch," Chuck would say. "You'll have to go back aft and get some." Or, "There's a box of cones up in the forepeak. Bring a couple of dozen down and put them by the rail at number seven hatch so the topmen can pick them up." Finally, one day half the lashing gang, while carrying cones aft, ran into the other half of the gang carrying cones forward. It turned out that Chuck was making a lot of unnecessary work for us. This was confirmed later when two men in the gang overheard a conversation from around the corner of a van between Chuck and the company superintendent. The superintendent remarked on how busy everyone seemed to be.

"Yeah, I like to keep everybody working," Chuck replied. Chuck was trying to make points with his boss, not by how much production he engendered, but how much work he had everybody doing. Once found out, Chuck's fate was sealed. Nobody would work for him. His were the last jobs filled at dispatch time. If there was no other work and you had to take a job at his pier, you made certain you kept your labor to a minimum that day. Finally, someone must have tipped off management. Chuck was taken off the ships and assigned to a walking boss's Siberia somewhere. I don't know if he was better off. I know that the lashing crews were, and production rose, of course.

In the past, doing work presupposed a need for it. It never occurred to anyone to create unnecessary tasks. In the preindustrial Middle Ages, the peasants worked the land, and when there wasn't any plowing or harvesting to be done, the peasants remained idle and free of sweat until something came up requiring their attention. Digging a hole in the ground in the morning so they had something to do filling it up in the afternoon was contrary to God's purposes. When the Industrial Revolution came along, however, and the peasant entered the factory, the factory owner knew how to turn their spare time into profit for himself. Idle hands do mischief find, so he initiated the twelve-hour day. It took more than 150 years of bitter struggle, but industrial workers finally achieved first the ten- and then the eight-hour day, and eventually the two-day weekend. The workweek we all presently put in to make our livings has been stagnant now for several decades, but with ongoing automation there is no reason it should not continue to drop. Actually, the time has come to inaugurate an indexing of the workweek, reducing the hours of toil based on the annual rise in labor productivity. It is only fair and rational that labor share in this gain, and it will make bargaining sessions between labor and management infinitely easier, in addition to doing away with the typical threatened strike every three years. Management's objections to this measure are sure to be shrill, with dire predictions of the catastrophic destruction of society. Their protests will have a familiar ring, one we have heard before. It is remarkably similar to their response to that first timid request long ago for relief from the twelve-hour day.

Labor productivity, the output of goods and services per hour of work per worker, is the prevailing yardstick against which all production is measured. It has become an iron rule of economics that productivity must always increase to maintain a nation's economic health. Those who subscribe to this theory, however, must live with and at the same time ignore the uncomfortable knowledge that it can never end, and furthermore that it must continue to accelerate.

Carried to its logical conclusion—racing to produce more and more goods with fewer and fewer workers—the paradox in this system of thought exposes itself for all to see. Unfortunately, this mode of production gets a bit shaky when the market stumbles over a lessening demand for goods and people are laid off work. Minus their usual income, those idle workers further injure the market by reducing their purchases, resulting in more layoffs. This spiraling down feeds on itself. Ultimately, every one of us who work for a living, whatever the color our collars might be, are potential victims of this economic system that gives power of decision over our lives to an authority that remains unchallenged.

Supported by the authority of think tanks in Washington, judges like the one in the Ninth Circuit Court of Appeals in San Francisco who ruled that an older employee, seniority notwithstanding, could be discharged if someone could be found to work more cheaply, and a multitude of others, the present system has imposed a situation where maximizing profits takes precedence over everything else, starting with human beings, and society's good health.

But perhaps my complaint is misplaced. Perhaps the failure of our present system is that it does not go far enough toward equality. If decisions of the kind we now live with were applied equally, then justice, harmony, and everyone's well-being might prevail. If no one were exempt—if there were no exceptions—to laws, law enforcement, and judicial rulings, everything would possibly work out smoothly. In the instance of this appellate judge, for example, perhaps we could then get someone younger, someone who would ponder and produce rulings for less money.

When work goes, to protest its loss is considered in many circles a failure to understand progress. To question this progress is simply to linger, if not wallow, in nostalgia for times past, for work gone forever. We are urged to get on the side of history and quit revering sweat. Worker's complaints are belittled and their criticism left unanswered. Automation, they know, has eliminated many blue-collar jobs, but shipping their remaining work out to Latin America and Southeast Asia is not automation, and questioning this "progress" has nothing to do with nostalgia.

History and evolution are not at work here. Economic class warfare is. Privileged self-interest is making an all-out assault on the American working class, both white- and blue-collar. Exporting jobs to China, for example, and then importing the product of those jobs back here cannot be supported by any economic argument. The balance of payments between China and the United States is presently five to one, $20 billion to $100 billion in China's favor. Those Americans involved in the China trade are selling a vital piece of our country—$100 billion of it—for $20 billion in return. That's okay with them as long as they get that 20 billion.

CHAPTER FIFTEEN

Living History

Workers' history, unlike other history, is not written down. At least not by the people who live and create it. That does not make it any less accurate. It simply means that it goes back only as far as the memory of the oldest living member of the working class and encompasses only the people and events he or she witnessed or were told about. Workers' history is also subject to failures, the same as any other history. While conventional history suffers from being written, and rewritten, by whomever's interest it is to rewrite it, worker's verbal history has a tendency to place individuals or groups in heroic roles when they perhaps behaved otherwise, like ordinary people, for instance. Everybody needs a hero now and then. Sometimes that is all that workers have got, or are left with, after a questionable victory, or an unquestionable defeat. So myths are created.

If you find someone who was actually there, however, you can usually get the straight facts, if you want them.

Fruit-tramps always held San Francisco longshoremen in high esteem. During a lettuce strike in Salinas, California, in the spring of 1936, the fruit-tramps were locked out, scabs were imported to do their work, and the National Guard mounted men with machine guns above the cabs of the trucks bringing in the lettuce from the fields.

The lettuce strike went on well into the summer. The Okies about this time had newly arrived on the California agricultural scene, and they got another lesson in hard economics. Many of them scabbed, but more of them did not.

After an initial burst of aggressive picketing, the packing-shed owners and the lettuce growers built a cyclone fence around their compound of eight or ten sheds, and patrolled it, inside, with armed guards. Periodically, the local police would swoop down and break up the picket lines, cracking skulls indiscriminately. The show of force was sufficient to keep all but the bravest strikers subdued. They may have had goon squads of their own, but ninety-five percent of the violence was initiated by privately hired thugs and municipal police in uniform, and one sheriff's department flying squad, which was particularly brutal. The lettuce strikers needed help, badly, especially with that sheriff's flying squad. Who to turn to? Where else but to those Frisco longshoremen 100 miles north who had won a hell of a strike two years before.

I know all this because as a twelve-year-old I saw the picket lines around the packing sheds and heard all the stories. My mother and father had been packing pears in northern California, and we drove through Salinas and spent a couple of days there on our way south to a tomato job somewhere or other down the coast. The fruit-tramps engaged in a lot of strikes in those times, but the strike in

Salinas remained noteworthy because it resulted, finally, in the formation of a union among the lettuce workers. And also because of those Frisco longshoremen.

The longshoremen's role in the strike expanded over the years. As a twelve-year-old, I had heard that they had sent money at the beginning of the strike, and later a couple of organizers had come down to help set up the union. I did not hear about the muscle until a year or two later. Many years later, while packing cantaloupes in the Central Valley, I discovered that three of my fellow packers had been in the Salinas strike. Had the longshoremen really sent down a gang to counteract the sheriff's goons?

"Yeah, they did," the man packing in front of me confirmed. "They came down and they kicked ass. I mean they kicked *ass.* " The four of us were putting on our gloves and aprons, preparing to go back to work after the lunch break. His friend nodded vigorously.

"Yeah, that they did," he said.

"I think they did," the third man said, nodding confirmation. "I never did meet them. But I heard they were there. And, you know, along about the second month of the strike they took them machine guns off the trucks and all the cops started behaving themselves better. Everybody said it was because of the longshoremen."

Many years after that I became a longshoreman myself. After ten years of working daytime, my partner and I decided to work nights for the summer. We made as much working four nights as we did working five days. School was out and we could spend more time with our kids, go camping, go to the beach, or merely work around the house. The night shift ends at 4 A.M. If you go immediately to bed when you get home, you can be up by ten-thirty or eleven, and you have the rest of the day ahead of you, or three or four days in a row, if you want to take a trip. My partner and I even joined a night-gang, bypassing the hiring hall and going directly to the pier at seven in the evening, which meant having dinner with the family at home.

John, our gang boss, was an old-timer. He had taken an active part in the 1934, 1936, and 1948 strikes, active enough to bring his thirty-thirty Winchester down to the waterfront and empty the weapon at a Coast Guard vessel escorting a boatload of scabs into Pier 48. John had a left hook, too. Once, while rigging gear, I saw him drop a man who started shouting at him in an argument over where to place the midship boom. I myself had no problems with John. My partner and I rather liked him. He knew more about long-shoring than we ever would. It was his gang. He could place the mid-ship boom wherever the hell he wanted to place it.

Someone had told John that I had once been a fruit-tramp. "Yes," I said in response to his inquiry. "I was a fruit-tramp. My mother and father were fruit-tramps. My sister still works at it."

"Ever work in Salinas?" he asked.

"Only once for a couple of weeks right after the war," I said.

We were tightening up the yardarm guy, taking up slack in the line. He was pulling down on the rope, giving it all his weight, and I was taking up the slack he gained by taking a couple of round turns on the cleat. "I never much liked working lettuce," I added.

"A bunch of the guys and I went down to Salinas once," he said. "It was in 'thirty-six. They were in the middle of a strike."

I was instantly alert. This was incredible. I was suddenly in a position to find out if all those stories I had heard were true.

"We went through there in 'thirty-six," I said. "I was just a kid. The National Guard had machine guns mounted on the cabs of the lettuce trucks."

"Yeah? Well, we didn't know that when we drove down there,"

John said. "It was a real wild goose chase." He and I finished securing the lines and retreated to the shelter of a deckhouse.

"I'd like to know what happened," I said. John was a closemouthed man. I hoped I was not appearing to interrogate him. But John talked on freely. What the hell, I was a member of the gang.

"There were two carloads of us," he said. "We had the address of this guy we were supposed to contact. They wanted us to take care of some company goons. Man, it was spooky. We timed it to get there just after dark. There was nobody on the streets except all these cops. We finally found the address. It was on a side street across the tracks. I went up to the door and knocked while the rest of the guys waited in the cars. Finally a man came to the door. I told him who we were. He turned white and slammed the door in my face. I went back to the car just as this black-and-white Ford pulled up with two cops in it. They stared at us and we stared back at them. Then the cop who was driving slammed the car into gear and tore off around the corner. We didn't know if they had a radio in the car, or not—most of them didn't in those days—but we didn't wait to find out. We took off out of there, too. Didn't stop until we got home and I dropped my guys off in front of the Ferry Building. Man, what a hare-brained scheme. No preparation at all. We could have got ourselves killed." I just looked at John. There was no question in my mind that I had gotten the straight story. I made a mental note to write my sister first thing in the morning.

After giving it some thought later, I decided that whatever the fruit-tramps believed, whatever truly happened, whatever history took place, those Frisco longshoremen had had one hell of an impact on the Salinas lettuce strike, more than the longshoremen ever knew. It gave a tremendous boost in morale to the strikers, and I think it might have given pause to a lot of the cops. When those two policemen pulled up while John was returning to the car, they were looking at ten real hard sons of bitches. I'm sure those cops spread the word.

Sometimes a lot of history can be covered by simple word of mouth. If a seventy-year-old tells a young man something that happened to him when he was young, and that young man recalls it when he is seventy, a good hundred years have been covered. Sometimes events only half as old can be startling. Once when I was very new to the waterfront—and working coffee, naturally—it started to rain. We quickly covered up the hatch and spread canvas tarps over it; one cannot permit coffee beans to get wet. One of the winch-drivers in the gang was an older, somewhat wizened, bent little man. He and I decided to go across the Embarcadero to a waterfront joint called Willie's until the rain stopped. Willie's had been there since the first earthquake. It did not have much to recommend it, other than it was close by, but it was warm and dry, and we were thankful to be in out of the rain. We each got ourselves a mug of coffee and sat down. The winch-driver had also gotten himself a jelly doughnut. He took a big bite out of the doughnut, chewed away at it, swallowed, and looked around.

"I never did much care for this place," he said, shaking his head. "When I first came to work on the waterfront my partner was shanghaied out of here."

"What?" I couldn't have heard right. "What did you say?"

"Yeah," he repeated matter-of-factly, "Shanghaied. It was nineteen fifteen." Being shanghaied—knocked out, kidnapped, and sold to some ship that was short of a crew—was something I had read about, but it happened on the Barbary Coast way back in another century. That's what I thought, anyway. Here was a man, alive and kicking, to whom in his youth it was an everyday walking around threat and danger.

"What . . . ? " I was at a loss for words. "Whatever happened to him?"

"Oh, he showed up about a year later. He'd been all over the Pacific and the Far East, until he managed to jump ship and work his way back here to Frisco." The old winch-driver chewed away on his jelly doughnut. I waited.

"English ship . . . ," he said between chews. "They were at war. We weren't yet. Hard to get a crew." He gulped. "Still raining?" he asked.

"Yes, yes, it is still raining. You want another cup of coffee?"

"Yes, I believe I do."

"I'll get it. How about another jelly doughnut?"

"You know, I think I would like to have another jelly doughnut. Here, I'll give you the money . . ."

"No," I said emphatically, jumping up. "I'll get it." I quickly got him another doughnut and a coffee refill. Outside, it looked as if it might be clearing up. I hoped to hell I could hear the rest of the story before we had to go back to work. He settled in, chewing away in silence on another jelly doughnut.

"Well . . . ? " I was becoming impatient. "I'd like to hear what happened to your partner"

"Nothing much more to tell. We, my partner and I . . . finished a ship . . . thirty-two hours in a row . . . used to work them straight through in those days . . . catch a couple of hours sleep, maybe, on top of the cargo out of the way somewhere." He took another big bite out of the doughnut. I waited while he chewed away.

"Okay. Where was I?" he said, finally.

"You'd finished a ship."

"Oh, yeah. Well, it was early evening. They paid us off . . . cash, in those days. We come in here for a drink. We each had a double. He wanted another one, but I wanted to go to bed. I was tired . . . very tired. I left. The next day I couldn't find him anywhere. Almost a year later he came dragging-ass in. Told me all about it. Some guy bought him a drink and that's the last he remembered. Next thing he knew, he was waking up on the deck of a ship, a freighter, going out through the 'Gate.' He was laying on a steel deck, and the Bos'n was slapping him on the soles of his shoes with a length of rope, telling him to get up and join the rest of the crew stowing gear." It had stopped raining. He gobbled down the last of his doughnut and we went back to work.

They tore down Willie's a few years back, to make way for a more genteel and upscale waterfront. At the time I felt they should have preserved something of it, if nothing more than a plaque on the sidewalk stating: "Men were shanghaied out of a saloon on this spot, pressed into service against their will so that ships might sail." A real historical monument, with pretentious language. On second thought I decided against it. Was that how I wanted longshore history remembered, with a plaque?

That old winch-driver had related to me that rainy day something that had happened forty-five years before. His story should have called for a celebration. In that forty-five years America had dramatically changed. The country had become civilized. No more were men drugged and kidnapped, spirited away from friends and family to endure long hours of hard work against their will. But now, forty-five years after that, what could I add to his story? That our country has changed? How? If that old winch-driver came back to life today, I would have to tell him that if an English ship needed to fill out a crew in Frisco now, they would not have to shanghai anybody. There would be two dozen men, and a few women, too, down there on the pier clamoring for the job.

CHAPTER SIXTEEN

The Road

Itinerant Americans providing crucial migratory labor are no longer a significant factor in our country's work scene. In agriculture there are no native fruit-tramps left in the West anymore, and those people working at harvesting crops up and down the eastern seaboard lack a common identity that binds them together as a group. They exist very close to the bottom in our society and, sadly, their various racial and ethnic divisions leave them fragmented to the point that they are unable to make demands as a united economic force. Their loyalties, although fierce, range no farther than their extended families; beyond that they have no cohesion. I have, for instance, heard of only one occasion when the various factions got together enough to go out on strike.

It was different once. Vagabond workers, coming to us in the nineteenth century from Europe where the custom had existed since the late Middle Ages, plied American highways and railroads as quickly as they were built. The highly skilled French mason, passed on by brethren from job to job and city to city, had several equally skilled occupational counterparts in America.

The printer-compositor offers a good example. So many of them were on the move well into the twentieth century that their transient status became institutionalized and accepted by editors, publishers, and printshop owners alike. The man's skill—they were all men— could be immediately authenticated by taking him back to the type cases and making him give a demonstration. That is, until the printing trades became organized into a union and banned all owners, editors, and foremen from the shop floor. Then he had to prove himself to a peer group, frequently a harder undertaking. The printer's coworkers, the journalists and news reporters, bounced around from job to job just as often, landing on one paper for a while and then departing for another almost on whim. Mark Twain, for example, worked on one paper in Nevada for only five weeks.

The vagabond worker, whether seeking adventure or merely in search of another locale, was always connected to work. It was work that made traveling possible. Work lay at the end of one journey, and the earnings from work made possible the beginning of the next. I used to know a true hobo fruit-tramp, now long dead, named George. Much of George's traveling was done by freight train. He was one of the few fruit-tramps who did not own a car. Although frequently he would bum a ride to the packing shed with me in the morning, I never felt he was sponging off me. He made it up in other ways. George never avoided work and certainly did not despise it. We worked together on a number of jobs, and he always packed a good crate.

Nobody rides a freight train anymore—probably because there aren't that many open and empty boxcars being hauled around the country these days—but when I knew him, that was George's preferred method of travel. I know this to be true because he proved it to me once when I offered him a ride to the next job in another town. It was fall, the melons were all through, and the tomatoes were about to start down south. George politely declined the ride. The next morning I saw him carrying his little yellow suitcase under one arm and a paper sack tied with twine dangling from the other. He was hotfooting it out to the edge of town to a railroad siding. Consequently, I once asked George what was so damned attractive about traveling by freight train.

"Oh, hell," George replied, coming to life, "being on the bum is a lot of fun . . . if you've got a little money." It was a way of life with George. I found it interesting that he had inherited that life, or rather, it had been passed on to him. His father had been a hobo, had lived and died a hobo. I was packing right behind George when he received word that his father had been found dead in a gondola car in Las Cruces, New Mexico. How the news was passed on to him I never knew, but it devastated George. He got drunk and blew the job. I did not see him again, and after a couple of years I began to wonder if George hadn't come to rest in some railroad siding, too. I brought it up with my father.

"George is up in Washington working in the apples. He pretty much hangs out in the Northwest these days," my father replied. I just hope George had something better than a boxcar to live in to escape those cold, rainy winters in the hill country around central Washington state.

If automation and the use of foreign workers has taken its toll of jobs from Americans, a changing society—History—has had an equally profound impact on work, workers, and work practices. George was a victim of all three. Much of the tomatoes today, for instance, are not picked or packed one at a time by hand. A machine, a self-propelled rig, moves down each row in the field and picks up the entire plant, tearing it out of the soil. The tomatoes, genetically engineered to ripen all at the same time, are then shaken from the vine onto a moving belt which deposits them into bins or cartons, depending upon what their final use is to be. For the Georges of the world, it is simply not possible anymore for them to hop freights and move around the country working here and there. First, the railroads will no longer tolerate it, and there are no cheap, working-class hotels left in small-town America to house transients. And no skid rows with cheap restaurants to feed them. Where these facilities still exist, the drug culture has taken them over. The tomato harvesting machine has a crew, of course, but it consist mostly of Latino workers, imported to do the work. They live out of town, close to the fields in cast-off mobile homes or cheap barracks. Small-town society prefers it this way. The alien workers are out of sight and come into town only now and then to buy groceries at the local markets. When the harvest is over, they head back south to Mexico.

Importing people to work in agriculture because they work cheaper always had a dubious ring to those of us whose jobs they took. How much cheaper? The last time I packed cantaloupes, which was a good many years ago, my labor added less than a third of a cent to the price of a melon in the supermarket, and I was making a thousand dollars a week. You get some idea of the skullduggery that goes into commerce when you consider that someone imported an alien to further divide up that penny.

Another reason given for importing labor, and not just agricultural labor, is that Americans, it is said, will not do hard, dirty, repetitive work, especially under onerous conditions, meaning, among other things, in the heat of summer when much of the harvesting takes place. Musing that over makes me wonder why so many fruit-tramps were willingly packing cantaloupes twelve hours a day down in Yuma, Arizona, in July.

When the demise of the fruit-tramps finally came, I was a bystander, but for years after I went to work longshoring, well up into the mid-seventies, I would leave the waterfront in the summer and for a month or so go back down into the San Joaquin Valley and pack cantaloupes once again. Although I did not gain financially, the move gave me a break from the waterfront and, as my kids grew into teenagers, I got them jobs on the packing sheds. Melons were the last foothold the fruit-tramps had in agriculture, but it was enough to give my three sons a glimpse of what their father, and their grandfather and grandmother, once did for a living. Even after I quit packing melons and remained working in San Francisco, my sons hung onto their summer jobs on the packing sheds. My oldest was the first to quit fruit-tramping. He became a plumber's apprentice and left the sheds for another trade. My two younger sons were still fruit-tramping when the final blow came.

In the mid-eighties the cantaloupe growers and shippers decided to do battle with the remaining fruit-tramps, drive them out of the industry, and replace them with people working for near minimum wages. Accordingly, when the labor agreement came to an end, they offered their shed workers an unacceptable contract calling for roughly a fifty percent cut in wages. The fruit-tramps rejected the offer, of course, and the strike was on.

In an almost classic scenario, the shippers and growers imported strikebreakers from wherever they could find them, and the fruit-tramps put up picket lines around the packing sheds in the four small San Joaquin Valley towns where they were mostly located. The corporate farmers had two advantages in the strike that they thought would give them victory: a cantaloupe had finally been perfected that would withstand the rigors of rough handling, requiring less skill on the part of the packer. The shipper's second advantage was a new, four-lane federal expressway, Interstate 5, that ran north and south the length of rural San Joaquin Valley. Cantaloupes that were not packed in the fields could be transported in bulk to central processing plants—huge, new, factorylike packing sheds, really—that were a new move in consolidating the industry.

Although fruit-tramps had been a summer fixture for over three generations in the small towns in which the strike took place, the local police, firmly under the control of the shippers, started pushing around the people on the picket lines. The fruit-tramps pushed back. My first knowledge of the severity of the conflict came with a phone call from my sister, out on strike at a packing shed on which she had worked for the previous seventeen summers.

"Tommy's all right," she said, skipping the hellos. Tom is my middle son.

"All right? What do you mean, all right? What the hell has happened?"

"They have felony warrants out for him and Don and about two dozen others," she said. Don was her son, my nephew. "They are hiding out right now. The union has a strike fund, so as soon as our lawyer gets here they will turn themselves in, and we'll spring them on bail. I called to tell you Tom is okay. I didn't want you to hear some wild tale from someone else."

"Wild tale? What wild tale? What happened?"

"The shippers were putting up this cyclone fence around one of the sheds. The posts they were using were two-inch pipes embedded in a puddle of concrete. The pipe was about ten feet long. The shed was working scabs, the concrete hadn't hardened yet, so Don and Tom and a bunch of others grabbed the pipes and, on the run, pole-vaulted up onto the deck of the shed and chased the scabs off in all directions."

"Oh, hell!"

"Well, you know the kids. They're going to be the first over the barricades."

"You're taking this pretty lightly. I guess no one was hurt?"

"Only the deputy chief of police. He's got a broken leg."

"That's serious."

"He says he was struck in the knee with a steel pipe. Everybody else says he broke it when he fell off the loading dock while trying to run away."

"I think I had better come down there."

"Everything is okay for now. I'll let you know if you're needed."

I was needed almost immediately by my youngest son, Marcus. The phone call came about dark the same day from Steve, another nephew, from another town about twenty miles north of where my sister was on strike.

"They've got Marcus in jail," Steve said.

"Oh, my God!"

"He's going to be arraigned tomorrow morning at ten o'clock."

"I'll be right down there," I said. I quickly calculated that I could make it in about two hours if I pulled out all stops driving. All I could think about was Marcus, barely sixteen years old, in a jail cell with I don't know how many goons working him over.

"It won't do any good," Steve said. "They won't even let you see him until tomorrow morning. And maybe you better bring along some cash for bail. We're running out of money."

Bail! Money! Cash! I needed cash. No banks were open. My friends! I would have to call friends. I would need money and lots of it. I also had to get control of myself. The idea of one of my kids in jail nearly drove me out of my mind. I thought back to our last longshore strike and how peaceful it had been. The shipping companies had not even attempted to use strikebreakers. We put up picket lines in front of the piers, and they remained unworked. My kids, young then, would come down when I was on picket duty and we would bat fungos around or play catch. Marcus was about eight years old, and all the longshoremen marveled at how far he could throw a football.

"How much, Steve? Any idea how much the bail will be?"

"Most of them were twenty thousand dollars. That's what mine was posted at, but we managed to get them reduced . . ."

"Twenty thousand!" I exclaimed. "That means two thousand up front . . . ten percent. What did you say? You're out on bail?"

"Yeah."

"What are you charged with?"

"They claim I incited a riot," Steve said with a laugh.

"What's Marcus charged with?"

"Somebody picked a scab off the loading dock with a rock."

"Marcus?"

"Probably. He always did have a pretty good fast ball."

Everybody down on the strike scene was taking everything so goddamned casual it was driving me crazy. My son was in jail. I wanted him out.

I spent a hellish night worrying about Marcus, although I rather easily and quickly raised over $2,000. Most working people have money secretly stashed away for emergencies, which they never use, usually. One large wad of cash came in, hand delivered about midnight, smelling earthy, like it had been buried somewhere in a backyard.

I called my oldest son, Ray—I simply needed some support. He took the day off work, and we got away early the next morning. The consequence of leaving early was that we arrived at the city hall and jail long before ten o'clock. Ray was driving and I was out of the car before he got it parked. I headed for the entrance to the city hall, determined to find out where the courtroom was and Marcus's place on the docket. And I ran into my son coming out of the building I was going into.

"Hi, Dad."

"Marcus! Are you all right?"

"Yeah, sure."

"We were told to be here at ten o'clock. What happened?"

"They stepped it up to nine."

"But you're free. Did they let you go?"

"No, I made bail."

"But . . . twenty thousand dollars?"

"I petitioned for implementation of Senate Bill twenty-eight."

"Huh?"

"Yeah. That reduced it to two thousand. It only cost me two hundred . . . ten percent." I was so relieved to see him I got the shakes. I had to sit down.

"Hi, Ray."

"Hello, Marcus. You okay?"

"Yeah, but I sure am hungry. Let's go get something to eat. All they give you for breakfast in there is oatmeal mush."

Unless there is a strict court order against it, it is mandatory that an arrested striker return to the picket line immediately to show the bosses you are not intimidated. Marcus figured he would return to strike duty at noon, so we had ample time to eat. Ray and I had breakfast while Marcus devoured an entire large pizza. Over bacon and eggs, Ray, also secretly relieved that Marcus was all right, gave his younger brother hell.

"The next time you bean a scab with a brick," Ray said, speaking from his own not-insignificant experience on a picket line, "make sure you're not photographed." There was a probability that Marcus was on film.

On the way back to the picket line after breakfast, Marcus insisted on stopping at a grocery store. He ran in and came out with three six-packs of sodas.

"We're picketing three gates," Marcus said. "I'm on the main gate. We'll go there last."

At the first gate Marcus was received with cheers. He dropped off one six-pack and we sped on. The second gate, at the back of the shed and out of the way, was manned by three big-bosomed, middle-aged farm wives, who had been picking up some summer money working on the sorting belt. They were holding down the fort under a beach umbrella. In the old days the local people working on the sheds usually did not go out on strike, but during this one they were true blue. They accepted the six-pack with a chorus of maternal clucking noises.

"Are you all right, Marcus?" one said.

"We heard you've been naughty, Marcus," said another, shaking her finger at him in mock criticism.

"Come back in about an hour, Marcus," the third one said. "We're going to have ice cream and cake."

The main gate, where all the action had taken place, was staffed by a serious group of veteran fruit-tramps. They quietly accepted the six-pack and gathered around my son to find out how he had fared. Ray said hello to a number of old friends, one of whom indicated a heap of stones on the ground.

"There's Marcus's rock pile," he said with a grin. He nodded toward the loading dock inside the fence about ninety feet away. "Ole Marcus really nailed that scab," he said to me.

The remark left me with totally mixed feelings. I knew, from my first strike when I was fifteen years old, that it was absolutely essential that you take out the scabs however you can. Otherwise you will not have an effective strike. But at the expense of my son doing time in jail?

On our way out of town, Ray and I stopped by the city offices; I wanted to get what information I could gather about Marcus's trial date. The scene at city hall was an outrage.

An entire platoon of special police—a Tac-Squad—was strutting around dressed in camouflage suits. Some of them were carrying automatic weapons at the ready. They were talking loudly and menacingly, obviously eager to go out and rip into a picket line. I could not imagine who had imported them, or from where. Did the mayor and chief of police of this small town not know that probably half the people out on strike were local citizens? Were they, for instance, going to send these crazies in uniform out to roust those three matronly farm women? Apparently, corporate agriculture had enough power to call in an armed force, and the local authorities did not have enough power, or did not want, to stop them.

Ray and I went back to the picket line, told them what we had seen, and then drove back to the city. But the day wasn't over yet. After I got home, a phone call informed me that, only minutes after I left, the cops went out and arrested Marcus again and threw him in jail on a different charge. The situation became even meaner. A few days later the sheriff and his deputies swooped down and grabbed a mother and daughter walking the picket line. They appeared the next morning shuffling into court in leg-irons with their wrists handcuffed to a chain around their waists.

Despite their huge losses—over half the crop rotted in the fields since they simply could not process the melons with inept help—the growers and shippers refused to seek any kind of a settlement with the people who worked for them over the years. Although their losses were substantial, they were diversified growers with large acreages in cotton, a crop subsidized by the government. This subsidy permitted them to absorb their melon losses and, of course, later deduct them from their income taxes. Many grew no melons the following year. When they did plant cantaloupes again, they packed them in the fields and used foreign labor.

It was the fruit-tramp's last hurrah. They lost the strike, and fruit-tramps were never employed in large numbers anywhere in the West again.

After it was all over, the charges against Marcus were reduced, and he was permitted to plead guilty to lesser charges and pay a fine. The local authorities in the other town pushed Tom's arrest to a conclusion, however. The union attorney managed to have the trial transferred to the county seat, a city thirty miles away, and postponed twice. Finally, one wintry day in late January, Thomas surrendered to a different sheriff there, spent the weekend in jail, and appeared in court Monday morning, where a friendly judge reduced the charge to time served and let him go free.

Sometime later I asked Marcus if he had learned anything, come to any conclusions about the strike. He thought the question over before replying.

"Yes," he said finally. "The next time I go out on strike, I'm going to recommend that all the pickets dress the same. Have everybody wear yellow T-shirts, for instance. That way it'll be harder for the cops to identify them, tell them apart."

I also learned something from their strike myself. If, in a future strike action in which I were involved, there were someone in a command situation who had kids on the picket line and violence was imminent, I would recommend that that person be immediately removed and utilized somewhere else, in public relations or wherever. If my experience was in any way typical, that person would be immobilized, unable to act, unable to think of anything but his or her kid's safety.

Although that strike was lost, and it marked the end of any large-scale employment of fruit-tramps in the West, some work remained on a small scale in out-of-the-way places. My mother's last job was packing spring tomatoes out on the edge of the desert not far from the Mexican border. I had taken out a travel card and was working in Los Angeles, putting her only a couple of hundred miles away, so the first chance I got, I drove down to see her. After leaving the main highway, I got lost on a series of dirt roads, and then a canal-tender directed me to the job. My mother and her friend, Vera, were packing two-layer flats in a little lean-to shed under a cottonwood tree, like it was a hundred years ago. The tomato patch was off in the distance beyond an irrigation ditch, ten, maybe twelve, acres of it. My mother and Vera could probably pack the entire crop if the weather stayed cool and the tomatoes did not ripen so fast that they came off all at once.

I drove up slowly, so as not to raise any dust, and parked the car. They were working away, their backs toward me, so neither Vera nor my mother were aware of my arrival. It was a typical country job:

two packers, four Mexican girls sorting the tomatoes into bins, and a handyman to nail the lids on the packed crates and stack them in the shade under the cottonwood tree. Both my mother and Vera had paper-racks attached to the sides of their packing benches and were wrapping, actually *wrapping* each tomato in tissue paper, like in the old days. The label glued to the end of the crates read DESERT GEM, and whoever grew the tomatoes had managed to get that brand name printed on the wrapping paper, too. All in one motion my mother and Vera were snatching tomatoes out of the bin, wrapping them, and placing them in the crate. They were making the wrapping paper "read" through a crack between the two slats along the side of the crate. Every tomato peeked out at you saying DESERT GEM.

My mother was so intent on packing those tomatoes that when I went up and tapped her on the shoulder, she jumped.

"Oh!" she said, dropping her hands into the crate in front of her. "What are you doing here?"

"I came down to see you."

"What for? Is anything wrong?"

"No."

"How are the kids?"

"They're okay. How come you are packing these tomatoes in flats? Nobody does that anymore. Everything is thrown into cartons now."

"Special order. All the little growers around here are doing a lot of it. They're going east . . . New York. We're about to eat. You want to have lunch with us?"

I hung around and my mother and Vera shared their lunch with me. But I ate mostly tomatoes. Spring tomatoes grown on the desert are the very best, tart and flavorful. Unless you've had one fresh, you can't imagine how good a tomato can be. Somebody in New York was in for a treat.

After lunch I pushed my mother aside and packed a few crates for her. She watched every move I made. Along the crack in the side of the box, I very carefully placed the wrapped tomatoes so they "read" all the way up to the end of the crate, just as she had done. After four or five crates, I could tell that my mother was getting impatient, so I gave her job back to her.

Two nights before in L.A., I had won $300 in a low-ball poker game. Before I gave her back her bench, I took out a hundred-dollar bill. When she wasn't looking, I slipped it in between the sheets of wrapping paper about a half inch down the stack—three or four crates away before she would run across it. Once in the car I had to back up in a hurry and get out of there. She was already on her second crate. When I turned out onto the farm road I took one long look back. My mother and Vera, two old ladies, were bent over their packing benches, working away, doing what they knew how to do best.

My father died in the lower Rio Grande Valley of Texas, down on the border. That country is subtropical, and in later years they started growing a lot of winter vegetables there. My father spent the last ten years of his life down on the Rio Grande, running crews of men packing lettuce in the fields.

My father had his own crews, and when he first went to Texas, he tried to introduce California ways to the lettuce fields, meaning he initiated piecework and paid the men for each carton of lettuce they packed. The going wage along the border in Texas when he first went down there was a dollar an hour. My father's crews were making two or three times that, and going home early. And then one day a delegation of farmers called upon my father. Either he paid the prevailing wage, or he was persona non grata in Texas. My father mended his California ways. Actually, he only modified them; all the field packers still wanted to work for him.

My father had a stroke, and before I could get down there, he was dead. The airline lost my luggage with my one dark suit when I changed planes in Houston, but I had transportation when I got down to the border because my father had an almost new pick-up truck. A good number of people came by his house to extend their condolences to me. There were even four or five old fruit-tramps whom I had not seen in years.

My father had remarked to me several times that he wanted to be cremated—he did *not* want to be buried. When I let this be known, his friends protested to the point of outrage. Okay. So we bury the Old Man. So what? I even put him on display in the small mortuary that took care of the burial, which resulted in another outrage.

"Look!" It was directed at me. My father, in his coffin, was in the center of the room. I was sitting off to one side. Four of the five old fruit-tramps were staring down at my father.

"What is it?" I asked, going over to the group.

"Would you just look at this?" one man demanded. "They shaved off his moustache!"

"Yeah," another put in. "What the hell do they think they're doing . . . shaving off Don's moustache?" I felt a twinge of guilt. My father had had a moustache almost all of his adult life. I hadn't even missed it when I saw him first laid out.

We were about to take Don out to the hearse when one final person, a Japanese American, showed up. He came running into the mortuary.

"Is Don dead?" he said in anguish. "Is Don really dead?" I took him over to show him my father, and then, largely against his will, roped him in as the sixth pallbearer. He then rode out to the graveyard with me in the pick-up. About halfway there he began to sob. He cried openly during the graveside services and during the whole journey back into town. I had known any number of Japanese American men over the years; the only time I had seen any of them cry was when they were drunk. He did not appear drunk. When we got back into town, he waved goodbye and jumped out of the pick-up at an intersection while the truck was still rolling. I never did get his name.

After we buried my father I hung around for a couple of days. I had not packed cantaloupes in South Texas in several years. This was winter, and different. It had rained, creating a lot of mud. After the second day I gave the pick-up to two of his oldest friends down there, a husband and wife, and flew home. I never did get my luggage. I attended the funeral looking like everybody else.

CHAPTER SEVENTEEN

Have Hook, Will Travel

Longshoremen on the West Coast of America have the prerogative of traveling up and down the seaboard to work in other ports. Every now and then when I got fed up with San Francisco and the old fruit-tramp within me called, I would take off and go somewhere else and work. If you are in good standing with the union, meaning, you are not delinquent in paying your dues, and the stevedore companies have no hold on you, which they practically never have (if you have been engaging in repeated on-the-job beefs, they are probably delighted to get rid of you), then you designate a port, fill out a travel card, and tank up the car with gas. For me it was a good feeling. I'm leaving town, heading for a new place, new people, and a job is waiting for me when I get there. Los Angeles, here I come. Or Coos Bay, Oregon. I liked working in Coos Bay, even though most of the work was loading logs, which you put together in bundles from rafts off-shore floating in the water next to the ship.

The first time I went to Coos Bay was in the early seventies, and I arrived under a cloud. The West Coast longshoremen had recently ratified a new five-year contract by the narrowest of margins. The new labor agreement, which was sponsored by Harry Bridges, was one of several dealing with automation. Many longshoremen, myself included, were opposed to the agreement. We felt that it threatened the hiring hall, that it gave back too much power over ourselves and our work to the employers. I, like many others, was vocal in my opposition, both in union meetings and on the job. After the agreement was approved—it took two ballots before Bridges got it passed—I decided to go off somewhere else for a while where life was simpler, and work in a different environment. I had no idea what I was getting into, working on the log-rafts, but I chose Coos Bay because I knew several longshoremen up there.

I took out a travel card, made a leisurely trip north, and arrived in Coos on a Thursday. The timing was important because Thursday evening was when that small local held its union meeting. As a courtesy, a visitor presented his travel card to the union secretary in the afternoon, and then attended the union meeting that evening where he was introduced to the membership. The Coos Bay longshoremen had one other custom they rigidly adhered to: the following morning the visiting longshoreman was escorted to the dispatch window and given the first job out, first choice of all the jobs in the port. That was the way it was in Coos Bay: if you were a visiting longshoreman you were a brother, even if they did not know you, and a fraternal welcome was what you got.

I checked in with the secretary in the afternoon, and presented him with my travel card. The secretary was aloof, somewhat cold even, in his reception, but I passed it off as having no significance, since I did not know the man. I attended the meeting that evening with Montgomery, my old partner from San Francisco, who had transferred permanently into the port. We took seats down near the front, to make it easier for me to be introduced, and waited for the meeting to begin.

Meetings generally started promptly at seven o'clock. By 7:15, however, nothing had happened. No one was even on the podium. Then a local longshoreman I knew from his having worked in San Francisco came down and tapped Montgomery on the shoulder, motioning Montgomery to come with him. I was left alone for perhaps a minute, then Montgomery came back, looking grim.

"Come with me," he said. I followed him out of the hall. Outside, a group of perhaps six or seven men were standing around in a circle. I knew all of them except for the secretary, who was in the center of the group. Montgomery took me up to the secretary.

"Tell him," he said to the secretary, "tell him what you just told me." The secretary looked uncomfortable. "Go ahead, tell him," Montgomery repeated.

"We had a phone call about you this morning," the secretary said, "from Harry Bridges."

"Harry Bridges?" I couldn't believe it. "You must be kidding. Harry Bridges?"

"Tell him what he said," Montgomery said to the secretary.

"Bridges," the secretary said, looking even glummer, "said that you were on your way up here to go to work. He also said that you were a fink, and a phony, and that you were out to wreck the union."

I was struck dumb. Although I later got acquainted with Bridges, I did not know him personally at the time, and I was surprised that he even knew who I was. It was like swatting a mosquito with a sledgehammer. There had been a lot of opposition to Bridge's automation contract, but I was about the least prominent of the longshoremen who came out publicly against it. If that opposition constituted a large pond, I was just about the smallest frog in it. Not too small for Harry Bridges to let slip by, apparently. I turned to walk away.

"Hey! Where you going?" someone asked.

"I'll see you later. I'm taking a hike," I said. "This is a Frisco beef. You guys don't need me bringing it up here."

"No, hold it," someone said. A couple of them actually grabbed me.

"No, you ain't going nowhere. You came up here to work, and you're going to go to work here."

"Thanks. Thanks very much. But I'd rather go. When this all blows over, I'll come back. Next year, maybe."

"No way," one of the men holding me said. He turned to the secretary. "He has an authorized travel card and he is a longshoreman in good standing. He came here to work, and he's gonna work."

"Okay, if that's the way you guys want it," the secretary said. He left and went back into the meeting hall. The rest of the group gathered me up and marched me back into the hall. They sat me down and stayed with me until the formalities of accepting a visiting longshoreman were completed. I went to work the next morning.

My going to work in Coos Bay was an example of longshore working-class principles prevailing over everything else. Coos Bay was a devout Harry Bridges port. In that small, isolated area, Coos longshoremen not only made almost twice as much money as other local working men, they had total medical and dental care, and vacation and retirement benefits that were unequaled. They felt they could not have done all this alone, and they gave Harry Bridges first credit for what they had achieved. In any contest between him and someone like, say, God, you would have done well to put your money on Harry Bridges. Except for a handful, every longshoreman in the Port of Coos Bay had voted for the contract, not because they approved of it, but because Harry Bridges asked them to vote for it. I got some cold stares during my stay there, but I was always treated fairly and correctly. Why did Bridges try to shoot me down? I never found out the reason. Many years later I served as secretary on a committee of which he was the chairman. His eyesight had begun to fail him, and I occasionally drove him home after our meetings. He would talk freely about anything I cared to bring up, but he never volunteered anything about his phone call to Coos Bay, and I never asked him.

That first morning in Coos Bay I took a job on a log-raft to work with my old partner, Montgomery. Everybody thought I was crazy because there were a number of easier jobs I could have chosen at the dispatch window. By midmorning I was convinced they were right. Until you get your "raft" legs, simply standing up straight on a floating log is a full-time job. No matter how still and rigid I kept myself, the damn log always began to rotate. I was wearing caulks (spiked boots) of course, but when I dug in to stop the rotation, the log simply started spinning in the opposite direction. And you weren't supposed to stand there; you were out on that log-raft to work, collect logs together, and build loads for the winch-driver to pick up and deposit down in the hold of the ship. After eight hours of this I was more than ready for dry land, to take a needed shower, clean up, and *sit down*. But even taking a shower became a problem; I had to reach out and brace myself to keep the walls from moving back and forth. After about a week I was okay, but the first few days were pure hell. It was extremely tiring, keeping your balance. I also got tired of being yelled at. When my log began to roll, I would abandon it and jump over onto someone else's log. The result was their log, due to my ineptitude, would shortly begin to spin, too. "Hey, Frisco, stay on your own damn log!" was the usual response. A couple of days before I left Coos Bay to return home, I finally achieved journeyman status on the log-raft. I realized this one morning when I ended up working with a brand new visitor to the port. He was from Los Angeles, and, consequently, answered to the name Pedro, from San Pedro, one of the ports down there. He had not gotten his "raft" legs yet, of course, and he was teetering back and forth, trying to balance himself with his pike-pole, as I had done. When the log under him finally spun out of control, he always seemed to leap over onto my log. "Hey, Pedro," I found myself yelling at him, "stay on your own damn log." I had already forgotten what it was like.

To outdoor people Coos Bay was a paradise. There was something wild from nature to eat the year around. You just had to gather it, catch it, or shoot it. Deer were hunted, of course, in season, and also quail (two kinds) and ducks, geese, and partridge. There were bear, if you wanted to shoot one. But bear was inedible, everyone agreed, although I once witnessed an argument during which a man insisted that "you could too eat bear meat." All you had to do was boil it for an hour and a half, pour off the water, then boil it for another hour and pour off *that* water. Then you ground it up with apples—three to one—and then baked it for forty-five minutes, like meatloaf. If you used a lot of catsup with it, he insisted, it was edible. Everyone else remained unconvinced. I do not know if he was telling the truth or not; although I ate everything else, I never tasted bear. Fishing went on the year around; there was always something in season. Also, digging for clams, and crabbing. You laid out traps for crab; big wire cages were sunk in the Bay with a punctured can of dog food tied inside. Then you anchored off somewhere and drank beer for two hours before going back and hauling them up. It was worth it. We took them to a friend's house, boiled them up, and ate them all afternoon. There's nothing like getting something free from nature that's good to eat.

The one wild food that had the most mystique attached to it was mushrooms. Mushroom grounds were sacred. Their location was secret. They were passed down from father to son, and the family plot, usually miles out in the woods, was never betrayed. I was invited by a local longshoreman once to go along with him on a mushroom gathering expedition, and it was made clear to me by everyone who heard about it later that it was an unusual honor. I was not blindfolded or anything like that, but on the trip out of town I became aware that a devious route was being taken. I woke up to the fact when I realized that we were passing an old barn for the third time. It was effective. I could not have retraced our route for the life of me. When it clouded over I even lost track of north and south. The trip back was even more carefully disguised. All for the gathering of the fabled chanterelle.

The various ports have their own "culture." I can think of no other word to describe them. Some ports are freewheeling, and almost anything goes. Others are very rigid and practice their own morality. In most ports, if the cargo turned out to be liquor, incoming or outgoing, the first thing the gang did upon opening the hatch was to crack open a case for their own consumption. One port in the Northwest, however, touched nothing, and more than one visiting longshoreman was sent home for drinking what to him was an innocent beer.

The different ports even have their own kind of humor, and in the usual blue-collar manner, it is turned inward on themselves. In the Northwest, where forest products are the principle source of work, the typical joke concerns someone losing his job to the conservationists, the "tree huggers": A game warden is driving along a back road near the coast when he hears a shotgun blast. He quickly parks his pick-up, creeps up, and peers over the nearest sand dune. Standing down on an outcropping of rocks near the water, a man is shooting seagulls. He has several laid out on a rock behind him. The warden stands up, boldly strides down, and confronts the man.

"You're under arrest," he says. He confiscates the man's gun, and picks up a couple of gulls for evidence. "Don't you know seagulls are protected? They're scavengers. They keep everything clean."

"Yeah, I know," the man mumbles.

"Well, why are you shooting them? What the hell do you do with them, anyway?" the warden demanded.

"We eat them," the man said, reluctantly.

"Eat them? My God! You eat seagulls?"

"Yeah," the man said, staring at his shoes. "Ever since the mill closed down and I got laid off work, me and the wife and kids have had pretty rough goin'."

"But seagulls?" the warden said, incredulously. "My God, seagulls! What do they taste like?"

"Oh," the man said, "they taste something like a cross between a spotted owl and a bald eagle."

In Los Angeles, where half the longshoremen are Americans of Mexican ancestry, the jokes take a not-so-different form: "Hey, how do you tell the best man at a Mexican wedding?" I was asked by a man almost as soon as I was introduced to him. His name was Sanchez.

"I don't know," I answered tentatively. "How do you tell the best man at a Mexican wedding?"

"He's the guy with the battery jumper-cables," was the reply.

Back home in San Francisco a few months later, I told the same joke at a party. It got a laugh, but a short time later a man came up to me and said that he had heard the same joke in a working-class bar in Gary, Indiana. Only it was a Polish wedding.

I have traveled north and south half-a-dozen times to work in other ports. Longshoremen, wherever they are on the West Coast, work under the same contract. They work the same hours and make the same hourly wage. Whatever their differences, and they vary enormously from port to port, they have at least one thing other than the work contract in common. When it gets down to the nitty-gritty, they can close ranks and act as one. Three years ago in Seattle when a business agent completed his term in office and went back to work, the stevedore companies tried to penalize him—not let him work— for the hard line he had taken while serving as an union official. From San Diego to the Canadian border, the longshoremen walked off the piers. The companies quickly reconsidered their position and let the man pick up his job. Then, and only then, did the rest of the longshoremen and women go back to work.

Chapter Eighteen

The White Male Worker's Dissent

As a blue-collar worker who writes on the subject of work and the people who do it, I have been asked repeatedly over the years why white, male, blue-collar workers have "deserted" the Democratic Party and, in substantial numbers, helped vote into the presidency Richard Nixon, Ronald Reagan, and the two Bushes. The question, if I have been collared by a liberal democrat, is usually asked in a hurt, accusatory tone—liberal democrats all feel they have a lock on the blue-collar vote.

I myself have given thought on occasion to how people mark their ballots, and I have asked the guys I work with and other working men how they vote, and why. I don't get much of an answer. They are reluctant to talk about it. It is a personal thing, but also my impression is that they, like me, feel ambivalent about almost everyone and everything they are asked to vote for, especially on a national level.

Starting with the New Deal in the thirties, the Democratic Party began a strenuous and admirable effort to pass legislation giving equality to labor under law and bring working people into the mainstream of American life. After World War II, when they had majorities in both houses of Congress, the Democrats, with the help of the Supreme Court, managed to achieve school integration, affirmative action, and gender equality: laws doing away with discrimination in hiring or promotion on the job. These were Democratic achievements and they were supported by a majority of Americans, white, blue-collar males included. At least at first. Later, almost all white, blue-collar males had reservations about what was happening.

Their reservations came when they discovered that there were fewer and fewer blue-collar jobs being created for these newcomer black and female blue-collar workers. In fact, by the middle sixties, with automation beginning to eliminate jobs at home, and then the further drain of employment opportunities resulting from factories fleeing overseas, the collective pool of blue-collar work was rapidly shrinking. White male workers discovered that the justice and equality that everyone was applauding was coming about almost solely at their expense. Not only were they being asked to share their customary work, which was okay with them as long as there was enough work to go around, but, when they became unemployed themselves, in many instances any new job they might have had was given, in preference, to a woman or a black. Being unemployed is no joke. Even if you have a job, very likely you have close friends or relatives who do not. If you have ever been out of work, or threatened with unemployment yourself, you know how these white, blue-collar men felt.

To make matters worse there was no one, in government or out, no mainstream organization of any kind these men could turn to which would politically plead their case. They couldn't even complain publicly. If they spoke out and said, "Hey, blacks and women are taking our jobs," they were publicly branded as racist rednecks or male chauvinist pigs. Even if the charges were true—and, with an issue as complicated as this one, blanket charges could only be partly true—they did not address the problem of these unemployed white men. The government's response to all this was to extend unemployment insurance and initiate job retraining. Retraining for what? Job retraining essentially became another way of extending unemployment insurance. I actually know blue-collar men in their forties who were retrained to become hairdressers. None of them made it into a salon, even though there was a demand for hairdressers. They simply had no talent for the work, except one guy I know who could give his wife a pretty decent frosty.

An equally destructive side effect of this loss of work to the blue-collar white male, employed or not, was that his sons had no place to go. In the past, blue-collar sons usually followed their fathers into whatever industry employed the old man. That became tough to do. They were white, too. Many sons, not finding work, wandered without direction through class after class at one community college or another, living at home well into their middle twenties or even longer, until a job of some kind turned up somewhere. Even if the kid finally landed on his feet, usually in a service industry, the continuity of the family and its concerns and traditions on into the next generation were frequently lost. Working-class ethics and culture are learned at home, but they are verified on the job and passed on there. The code of conduct workers define for themselves comes through working with each other and sharing the demands that the factory, mill, or mine makes on them at work. While acknowledging the unfairness of the old days, no old-timer I know has anything good to say about the way new workers are hired into his industry. Call it nepotism if you like, but many of the longshoremen I know continue working on toward retirement with the disappointment that they have no son working with them who will carry on after they are gone. I haven't the slightest idea how they vote, but self-interest here becomes pretty cloudy.

If voting is a personal, somewhat private, thing among the workers I know, those who don't vote can get downright hostile when asked. Everybody is supposed to vote; that is the message we are endlessly bombarded with.

"You voted yet?" I asked an acquaintance on the day the Gore-Bush debacle was about to take place.

"Who's to vote for?" he demanded.

His vehemence prohibited me from replying lightly with something like, "Well, if you don't like the candidates on the ballot you can always write in yourself."

"Gore or Bush?" I said finally.

"Fuck 'em both!"

End of conversation. There was anger in his reply, so it had to be a political statement. The best explanation I can come up with for his response is an analogy to race: If you were a black American living in the South, or anywhere else, for that matter, and the only candidates running for office were two white racists, why the hell should you bother to vote for either?

Poll samplers, hitting on people leaving the voter's booths in Midwest working-class districts in the Gore-Bush election, claimed that a bit more than half—fifty-two percent—of the white males interviewed said they voted Republican. What is significant here is that if the Republicans got a little over fifty percent of the vote in an election with only a fifty percent voter turnout, then almost three-quarters of the people eligible to vote did *not* vote for them. Approximately the same can be said of the Democrats. That is not what one could call a mandate to power for either party.

People who don't vote range from those who disenfranchise themselves by indolence and lack of interest in the whole process to those who don't want to go out in the rain to get to the voting booth. And then there is the man and those like him who say, "Fuck them both." How their numbers break down is anyone's guess, but the significance of the people who choose not to cast ballots is that they are determining the outcome of elections in America, and their numbers are increasing annually.

In the last election, Gore, almost contemptuous of labor, reiterated his approval of the ongoing Democratic platform of supporting NAFTA, the World Trade Organization and its fostering of support for the exporting of blue-collar work to foreign factories, and, finally, raising the immigration quotas permitting the importation of more foreign labor, all measures detrimental to American working people. What makes these "fuck 'em" nonvoters so angry is that if they had voted Democratic, had voted for Gore, they would have been participating in their own destruction, actively subscribing to their own demise.

Political parties, it can be demonstrated, come into being in a democracy to represent existing class interests. With the working class in America becoming less and less represented over the years, why did not a labor party of any significance come into existence in this country? Part of the blame, of course, lies with trade-union leadership. The AFL-CIO superstructure felt an ongoing compulsion to subordinate the interests of their constituents, the workers, to fulfill what they saw as a more vital need: to keep the Democratic Party intact and in power. Another diversion, unquestionably, was the rapid rise, and even more rapid rejection by labor, of the Progressive Party in the election of 1948. But in the following fifty years, with the need for labor representation becoming increasingly more pressing, no political party or organization has come into being to fill this void.

Could a mainstream labor party have gained acceptance and the ongoing support of the working people of America during this or any other time? There is evidence to indicate that the answer is yes. In 1920 Eugene V. Debs, running from prison on a socialist ticket, received almost a million votes for the presidency. Twelve years later, in 1924, Senator LaFollette of Wisconsin, running on a pretty much similar program, received almost five million votes. In 1992 Ross Perot, running not so much *for* something as he was running *against* the two major candidates, persuaded twenty million Americans to vote for him. Obviously those twenty million ran the gamut from liberal to reactionary, but they do indicate the number of disgruntled voters willing to abandon the two major parties.

It has been maintained, repeatedly, that three political parties are inimical to the functioning of the American democracy, to the successful working of its unique legislative processes. This has been put forward as a solemn truth by the two existing major parties, as if their self-interest had no part in keeping things the same as they are. Third parties, they maintain, do nothing so much as muddy the electoral waters. They are correct. Ross Perot in 1992 probably took the presidency from George Bush senior and placed it in the hands of

Bill Clinton. And in the election of 2000, Ralph Nader, with a mere two million votes, gave Bush junior an electoral victory. Clearly a third party can have a major impact on politics in America. A labor party, with candidates for Congress in addition to the presidency, with an all-inclusive pro-labor platform, representing white-collar labor, too, would have ongoing positive results far greater than they can presently claim for their constituency.

The question remains, Could a labor party have gained power in America as it has, twice, in Great Britain, and in most of the other democracies in Europe? One cannot say for certain that it would not have. But even if it had not, a minority party, a genuinely American third-party presence representing labor, could at many times over the past fifty years have represented a balance of power between the two other parties and successfully made demands in labor's interest. Certainly the workers would have fared no worse than they have over the past five decades. A labor party would also have gone a long way toward uniting what is now a fragmented work force. Instead of *black* workers, *female* workers, and other categories now placed in competition with each other, everyone who labors for a living could begin thinking of themselves in terms of what they all really are, workers, pure and simple.

CHAPTER NINETEEN

Labor Law and the Worker

I have twice been indicted as a racketeer by the United States government. Except for being paid by my local to represent it on union business, usually for a week or two once a year, all the money I have received over the years on the waterfront came from working the ships. (I have, of course, received money occasionally from my writing, which is incidental.) I make this disclosure to lend credence to my plea of innocence. How then, you may ask, could I, an honest man, be charged with such an heinous crime? Unquestionably, a rare and terrible mistake must have been made. Rare? Twice? In both indictments other rank-and-file longshoremen were named indiscriminately along with me. We were all charged with extortion. We put up a picket line to protect our jobs; the extortion occurred when we demanded existing longshore wages for working them. How could these charges against us possibly come about? The answer lies in how labor laws have been written, enacted, and enforced in America over the years.

My first indictment as a racketeer occurred because I was an officer of record (vice-president) when our union picketed a pier where they were attempting to load and discharge cargo by using non-longshore personnel to do our work. The second indictment involved a picket line too, but it was a bit more complicated. The largest steel company in America had contracted with a South Korean steel concern to process and ship stock steel to the United States and discharge it at a Bay Area port. The American steel company had determined that they could save money over their domestic smelting operations by buying foreign steel, shipping it here in foreign ships, and then save even more money by using unskilled, non-union longshoremen to unload those ships, for half our wages, of course. We decided we weren't going to stand still for it and threw up a picket line.

The place chosen to discharge the incoming steel made picketing difficult. The pier was in the northern Bay where it joins the river, and the installation was so large and isolated that we could not set up an effective picket line—not by land, anyway—so we decided to picket by sea.

A longshore friend of mine, Dan, owned an old tugboat. It was his pride and joy. When Dan wasn't working as a longshoreman, you could always find him aboard his tug, tinkering with one thing or another. Early one morning Dan, with another crewman named Colin and me, took the tug out to meet the very first vessel to come in with a load of steel to our port.

We had stretched a large sign across the bridge of the tug, identifying it as a picket boat. When the vessel came in, it had to change pilots for the run up to the river, so we raced ahead and were waiting for it when it arrived at the new steel dock. In all we had three other picket boats in the water in addition to the tug, an inflatable, a small cabin cruiser, and a fish boat. The inflatable promptly ripped itself open on a snag, and the cabin cruiser got itself stranded on a sandbar, leaving the picketing to our tug and the fish boat. We were not alone, however. Also waiting at the steel dock were five Coast Guard boats, one or the other of which was constantly pulling alongside of us and, using a bullhorn, threatening us with all sorts of dire consequences if we became a hazard to navigation. We played a cat-and-mouse game with them for almost two hours, not actually preventing the steel ship from docking, but making it awkward to do so. Finally, very adroitly, Dan and the fish boat maneuvered around until one of the Coast Guard boats found itself between the big vessel and the dock. This gave the pilot aboard the ship the excuse to abort the entire operation and take the vessel back down to the Bay, where it lay swinging on its anchor for two weeks. We celebrated our victory—a temporary one, it turned out—by breaking out a case of beer and setting a leisurely course for home. The next day pictures of the heroic tug appeared in all the papers. The day after that, we seagoing pickets had to appear in the municipal court of the town nearest the steel dock to answer a charge of unlawful assembly. A month later Dan, Colin, and I, and a number of others who weren't even there, were named in a federal indictment and charged with the Racketeer Influenced and Corrupt Organizations Law, the RICO Act.

All charges were eventually dismissed, of course, but not before a great deal of money was expended by our union in legal fees defending us. The membership, who ended up footing the bill, supported us all the way, as they always do in conflicts of this sort. The costs of the picketing and its aftermath were not limited to money, however. A number of longshoremen named in the indictment were uneasy during the proceedings, and they had a right to be. If the steel company had made the charges stick, they could have gotten a judgment against them and seized and sold these longshoremen's homes to settle it. I was pretty much immune to that threat because I don't own a home, I rent. But Dan could have lost his tug. That would not have deterred Dan, however; he would have rammed that steel ship if he thought it would have done any good. In Colin's case, it broke up his marriage. His wife understood what was happening, why it was happening, and the unfairness of it all, but a federal indictment by the government of the United States of America? It was still shameful, and she would just as soon not be married to a man who placed himself in a situation where he would be exposed to such a charge.

The indictment confused a lot of people and that was exactly what it was designed to do. But, if it were impartial, why would our government impose this situation on us, workers ask themselves. RICO, the Racketeer Influenced and Corrupt Organizations Act, was not supposed to be put together to harass workers trying to protect their work. As a matter of fact, RICO, the Taft-Hartley Act, the Landrum-Griffin Bill, and all the fine print contained in these measures were landmark labor legislation designed, we are told, to protect American citizens, especially the working stiff. How then did it come about that blue-collar workers almost without exception regard these laws as anti-labor? A couple more examples might explain why.

The Taft-Hartley Act of 1947 made a provision for a ninety-day "cooling off" period to delay a strike, let both sides, labor and management alike, think it over while continuing to negotiate toward a settlement. This procedure is put into force by petitioning the Department of Labor. Either of two parties can initiate it, the federal government or management. In theory, labor could initiate this measure, but they never do; have you ever heard of management going out on strike? Consequently, over the years the "cooling off" provision of the Taft-Hartley Act has become a device management uses to keep production going while postponing settlement—they can always find a judge who will give them the ninety days. This has given management slack that labor does not have. They have the option of using the ninety days to build up their inventories in preparation for a strike, or, if management has weakened its labor force to what it thinks is beyond recovery, they can choose not to use the ninety days, precipitate a strike, bring in scabs, and hope to break the union, bringing an end to the trade union local involved.

What workers discern from all of this is that whether they go out on strike or not, and when, is largely determined by forces hostile to them and other workers.

Knowledgeable people sympathetic to labor invariably blame the courts for the outrages practiced against workers under the Taft-Hartley Bill, and it is true that big industry can always find a judge who will use it to give them a restraining order against labor, backed by enormous and expensive penalties if violated, whenever management decides they need one. But the two reigning political parties are as much to blame as the courts. They enacted these laws, and even though Democratic legislators insist that they did not support them, this plea is suspect. After all, the Landrum-Griffin Bill of 1959, which essentially only refined and extended the Taft-Hartley Act, was originally entitled the Kennedy-Landrum-Griffin Bill until J.F.K. decided it was politically unwise and had his name removed from the measure.

Workers mistrust legislators, their laws, the judiciary who interpret them, and the police who enforce their rulings. Workers do so because their observations and experience over the last fifty years have led them to this conclusion. Any objective examination by a disinterested party of labor legislation since the Wagner Act of 1935 (which genuinely attempted to empower blue-collar workers so they could become an equal and functioning part of American society) could only lend weight to their conclusions. Individual workers may only have vaguely heard of this subsequent legislation, but they know of its existence and regard it as just another law to be used against them, which is confirmed every time they open a newspaper and read an account of the problems a body of workers just like them are having who have gone out on strike somewhere in America.

The recent ruling of the judge of the Ninth Circuit Court in San Francisco, stating that an employer could dismiss all established rules of seniority and discharge an older worker if the employer could find someone who would do the older worker's job for less money, is the latest case in point. How could any worker regard this as other than a hostile threat to his work and well-being?

CHAPTER TWENTY

Blue in America

There will always be blue-collar work in America, of course, however much of it is eliminated by whatever means. In those factories and workplaces that have not disappeared lock, stock, and barrel, there will be workers who remain to do the work that remains. Additionally, those still holding jobs after automation has been introduced will most likely profit by their survival. Having reduced the payroll, the employers can afford a substantial pay raise to those left—it was probably even part of the deal. But this good fortune will be tempered for many by the sober realization that their present job now has an increased workload, brought about in part by taking up the slack of the workers who are no longer there.

It is imperative that those workers left after the cuts have taken place contractually nail down the new manning scales—who does what and how many workers are needed to accomplish the job—because after a brief pause management will start looking for places to trim again. I got a frank admission of this once when in a joint labor relations committee meeting with our employers. A new work agreement had given the employers the right to use a reduced number of longshoremen in specific work situations. The ink was barely dry on the agreement when the employers attempted to extend reduced manning measures to all longshore work in the port. As vice-president of the local, I sat in on the meeting.

It was the late seventies. A new agreement had been signed in July. It was now September, and in that brief time all sense of waterfront harmony had evaporated. In many of those areas of work where we had agreed to the introduction of machinery to replace longshoremen, the operations had remained unchanged. The employers were simply pushing to get the same amount of work done with half the men. The men pushed back by dragging their feet. The employers screamed slowdown and demanded a meeting with us to get their moves validated. To compound the problem, the representatives of the employer group sitting across the table from us were submitting new demands to modify the agreement, using as authority a review clause in the contract. They wanted even more cuts in the manning scale, and if they did not get them, they were threatening to take the issue to an arbitrator, which would be a dicey situation at best. The arbitrator would probably give them at least part of what they wanted. The president of the local was the speaker for our group, but I'd had about enough.

"You guys are too much," I burst in. "If you managed to reduce the number of men working a ship to two longshoremen, you'd immediately try to get rid of one or the other of them."

"Why, yes, of course," the leader of the employer group replied in all innocence. "That's our job." We longshore representatives had to resist an urge to just get up and march out, telling them to go fuck themselves. We hung around long enough to say *NO!* Longshore work cannot be exported, but I have no doubt that if it could have been arranged, our employers would have been shopping around to get our work done overseas.

As it turned out, this particular controversy was settled informally, as are so many beefs that come up on the waterfront. The employers had to get their ship loaded out, and the rank-and-file longshoremen were threatening to take over and settle the dispute themselves. Maybe a few ships wouldn't sail. The employers backed off, and the men acquiesced in some of the new procedures with the tacit understanding that they were the ones who loaded the ships and, however they did it, the work would get done, and the employers would refrain from intruding into traditional work practices. It was a pretty cold work situation for a while, but things finally settled down.

Other work in other industries still remains with us. A new house going up cannot be wired for electricity, have its roof put on, or its plumbing installed in the Orient. This, in addition to their skills, is one of the major reasons the organized building trades workers have stayed healthy and continue to make decent wages. The biggest threat to carpenters is that there is always a multitude of wood butchers around hoping to shove some journeyman aside and work for less money. Teamsters, also, are not without problems. It is relatively easy to buy a tractor, the power unit of a semirig, and haul vans and containers around the country. It is so easy, in fact, that the unorganized drivers, by placing themselves in competition with each other, have driven their earnings down to the level where only a few of them are making a decent living. Longshoremen on the West Coast are somewhat better off. Strong trade unions can be destroyed, as they repeatedly have been in the past, but the Coast longshoremen, in addition to being strongly organized, are strategically placed. They have also discovered that automation and the changing cargo handling methods that so decimated them can also be used to their advantage.

Before the introduction of the container ships with their oceangoing vans, the shipping and handling of cargo remained essentially unchanged for centuries. Whether it was steam, sail, or a Roman galley, the cargo was loaded by hand, piece by piece, aboard ship in its port of origin, and discharged the same way when it reached its port of destination. Once discharged, the cargo was drayed, either by diesel truck or an oxcart, to a warehouse and stored to await distribution. All port cities warehoused enormous quantities of cargo up and down their waterfronts, sometimes for extended periods. In our port, for instance, cargo destined for the Christmas trade started piling up in early October. With the container, all that changed. The big warehouses found in our larger port cities became obsolete; indeed, most of them have now gone retail and become the repositories of chic shops and restaurants trading on the romance of their maritime past. Today there are essentially no warehouses left on the waterfronts for the storage of overseas goods, coming or going. The mobile container has become the warehouse of today, and everything is in transit.

It takes six to eight weeks for a television set manufactured in Japan to reach a store and go on sale in Denver, Schenectady, Pittsburgh, or wherever. Ships usually cross the Pacific in three weeks. After the vessels reach our shores and are discharged, the haul and distribution of goods across America, either by train or by truck, can take another two or three weeks, rarely longer. This flow is constant, and it is very precisely maintained. Those T.V. sets must arrive at point of sale *just in time*. After all, the store has no warehouse and does not want merchandise on hand that will not sell immediately, or at least by the end of the week. Equally, they do not want to tie up their capital in inventory. There cannot be a shortage of goods, but if the cupboards are bare, the store has nothing to sell. This very delicate balance, once finely tuned, has to remain intact. If the Coast longshoremen interrupt this flow of goods for three days, or even less, everything starts to go to hell. Shut it down for a week and disaster threatens. Thus, automation, although it devastated the longshore ranks—in San Francisco alone a workforce of five thousand men was reduced to one thousand in less than twenty years—it also brought with it an unwelcome surprise to the ship and stevedore company owners. Those workers remaining on the waterfront became potentially more powerful. They could tie up the entire continent.

The last major strike on the West Coast waterfronts took place almost thirty years ago. At that time the seagoing container was just being introduced, and the bulk of the cargo was still being discharged and loaded by hand. The enormous impact of the vans had yet to be felt in full in the industry. Since no strike takes place in America without a secret vote of the workers involved, the ship owners had hopes of exploiting this new system without longshore participation. At the time, the longshoremen did not fully understand the impact that the vans would have on their lives, but they knew that they had better not be left behind when decisions were made affecting their work. Consequently, 97.5 percent of them voted to strike and promptly walked off the ships. Every port on the West Coast was shut down. One hundred and one days later the federal government, invoking the Taft-Hartley Act, mandated a ninety-day "cooling off" period, and everyone went back to work. Three months later everyone went out on strike again. The second strike vote saw a drop to only 93.5 percent in favor of hitting the bricks again. Thirty days later a contract agreement was arrived at, and the strike was over.

On the face of it nothing very important was gained. All the newspapers, which had been describing us in condescending terms, like we were naughty boys, now decided we were also stupid. We longshoremen had gone out on strike for four months for a pay raise the ship owners would have given us on the first day of the work stoppage. Among the employer group, however, there was no laughter. There, wiser heads digested the reality of their situation and decided that strikes, or lockouts, were no longer a permissible option for them; some other method had to be devised to keep their industry functioning. What they finally decided was to simply purchase labor peace. Management unquestionably hated to do it, but in the end it was not only effective but probably cheaper. They financed a series of pay raises by passing on the costs to their customers and by cutting manning scales on the waterfront to the bone wherever they were strong enough to do it.

Using figures released by the Pacific Maritime Association, the employer group, the average longshoreman on the West Coast of America made approximately $77,000 in 1998, putting them close to par with the salaries of the executives in the industry. So far this has brought labor peace. Some longshoremen unquestionably feel that they are making too much money to ever go out on strike again, especially those earning more than $77,000. But 77,000 is average, and like all averages, it can be deceptive. Half the longshoremen earn below that figure, and a significant number make considerably more. In the upper range—keeping in mind that a five-day week adds up to working 2,000 hours a year—those longshoremen working 2,800 hours a year, seven days a week, made $124,185 for the work they did in 1998. That means working the whole year and al-most every day of it, Saturdays, Sundays, and all holidays except for Christmas and the New Year, when the waterfronts are all closed down.

What kind of a person does it take to work like that? One would presume them to be rare. As a matter of fact, 14.8 percent—over one in seven—of the Coast longshoremen worked 2,800 hours or more in 1998. Another 19 percent worked over 2,400 hours. Who are these people? I know a number of them. Most of them are young men and women with growing families who are attempting to pay off a home they are buying. Some of them aren't so young, like those try-ing to put kids through college.

On the bottom of the scale are those who worked fewer than five days a week, including those who put in four days, three days, or even less on the job. These people totaled a remarkable 44 percent of the longshore workforce. Among longshoremen, apparently almost half of them, if given the opportunity to choose between accruing more money or spending more time at home pursuing private inter-ests, opt for the latter. Who are the people that constitute this group? First of all, its membership is always in flux. The young person tak-ing on a heavy workload because he has just bought his first home might lighten up once the mortgage is paid off or he gets the house payments under control. Essentially, the people working less are those whose life situation has arrived at a point where they can get by and live comfortably on less money, and they *choose* to do so. Forty-four percent does not accurately describe their numbers. Probably twice that many work an abbreviated workweek and pass into this group toward the end of their longshore careers. Lucky of them to have this good fortune? Luck and good fortune have nothing to do with it. Their strategic location helps, but it is their awareness and use of their organizational strength that has enabled these workers to create this work situation for themselves. In doing so they also reveal a startling difference between working-class and middle-class values, and prove once again that class distinction is still very much alive in America.

As blue-collar workers enter middle age, their job seniority permits almost all of them to claim positions that give them some relief from the toil, stress, and responsibilities of the high-powered areas of the workplace. This is approved of, thought only right, and looked forward to by the younger workers. The white-collar worker, on the contrary, is on a track to succeed, and success is defined by promotion. When he enters middle age, he is expected to be coming into his own, entering into the period where his greatest effectiveness and productivity will take place. If he fails to achieve and does not attain his proper executive station, he is deemed a failure, and from that time on he can only look forward to a gradual loss of status and stagnant earnings. He is a supernumerary for the remainder of his career, unlike the blue-collar worker who, unencumbered by the built-in drive and ambition that the white-collar worker is pressured to embrace, is respected, and his prestige increases as he advances toward retirement.

The Pacific Maritime Association, the employers, by and large have to accommodate themselves to the way longshore workers work. But the work gets done. It may appear that the PMA does not have a choice, but that is not true. They simply do not have the choice of becoming a tyrant and imposing their will on their workforce. Unfortunately most workers other than longshoremen in America cannot assert themselves in this manner. Their bosses determine their workload and how and when they do that work, throughout the day, every day of their working lives.

What is the attitude of the employer group, the Pacific Maritime Association, toward their employee's work habits? Actually, they have matched their production process to the reality of the situation and, curiously, they have no complaints about that percentage of their employees who hit it hard and work seven days a week. Indeed, one of the principal complaints of the PMA is that too many longshoremen do not work enough. To this end they permit longshoremen to forego their prepaid vacations and holidays and work through them if they choose, in a sense collecting double time for the equivalent of up to six or seven weeks a year. They would like to see everyone down there on the waterfront working their butts off every day apparently, and this is just one of the "rewards" ship owners take to bring this about. To their credit, their primary instrument is the carrot, not the stick. In an industry where the worker's wages are among the best in the country, they offer them, what else, more money. The last contract, for the first time in the history of West Coast longshore agreements, contained a 401(k) savings plan. Matching funds for up to $2,000 a year are offered to the individual longshoreman. I do not believe, however, that this will induce those longshore men and women who are presently working three- and four-day weeks to mend their evil ways and take on a larger workload. There have always been opportunities to earn more money on the waterfront, but with almost half the workforce at any given time deciding that private pursuits are more important than more money, it is unlikely anything will change.

Longshore workers are no different than other blue-collar workers in America. Unfortunately, not many other laboring people can gain the advantages longshore workers have. Which leads one to conjecture, what if they could? What if all the workers in the United States, white and blue collar alike, had adequate wages and the choice of working only to fulfill the need of maintaining a comfortable life? What would America be like if a majority of its citizens remained unresponsive to the lure of accumulating superfluous wealth and property?

After describing these aspects of longshore life, however, it must be said that working on the waterfront is not all a soft touch. There is nothing leisurely about making a living as a longshoreman on the West Coast. The work gets done at very close to breakneck speed, with the machine dictating the pace. Even with the longshore workers having the power to enforce a less hurried routine, they usually do not. Collectively, they subscribe to the age-old dictum of getting the ship loaded as fast as possible and on its way back out to sea. There are incentives, of course. When the longshoremen turn-to at 8 A.M., they are guaranteed eight hours' pay. If they can get the ship out in six or seven hours and go home early, they still get paid for eight hours. That is just one of many tacit agreements between the men and the boss, and one the boss had better not violate or all sorts of unpleasant events will occur, starting with the next ship failing to get loaded out on time and having to lay-over an extra shift before sailing. If this is a severe system, it also has its advantages for the boss. Longshoremen usually work in pairs or in teams. If there is a recalcitrant worker present on the job, the boss does not have to enforce discipline. The workers do it among themselves because the slacker is not carrying his share of their collective load. Some bosses regard this as an infringement on their jurisdiction and their role in life—how else is a boss to define himself if he doesn't get to boss people around? If a boss has a problem with that, it is his alone. Some of the waterfront boss's choices are deliberately restricted for basic reasons of equality; he does not, for instance, get to choose his workers, but employs those people sent to him from the hiring hall. Waterfront democracy dictates that longshore men and women get to choose their jobs from those remaining available to them when it is their turn at the dispatch window. And the system works. Although maritime executives will argue otherwise, an examination of man-hours to tonnage output indicates that West Coast production figures are above average worldwide. And however much longshore wages and fringe benefits have increased over the years, they have been more than justified by increased production due to automation. A look at labor costs to load and discharge cargo from ships indicate that they have remained essentially unchanged for the past thirty years. In other words, the cost of loading a ton of freight today is the same as it was three decades ago. West Coast longshoremen meet the hook when the crane driver brings in the cargo. If it is a container, when he lands the van, they lash it down with speed and efficiency. Although they rarely verbalize it, they firmly believe that the gains of automation, the returns from increased production, do not belong solely to the stevedore companies, the ship owners, and their stockholders.

The last two centuries especially have seen bitter struggle and conflict the world over for workers. Although very few West Coast longshoremen profess any particular ideology, they moved collectively sixty-five years ago to restructure how work was done in their industry. Fairness demanded that they share the work equally. That same sense of equality then insisted on interchangeability; when a longshoreman goes up to the dispatch window, he has a choice of any job available that he or she feels he or she can handle. Workers become interchangeable without losing their identity and becoming a mere cog in the industrial process. If a skill job becomes available to him through seniority, he becomes eligible for skill training. Some facets of this work ethic have been lost in recent years, but the right of choice remains. Not only the choice of jobs, but the further choice, when you can afford it, of absenting yourself from work. To work or not to work then becomes the question. With adequate wages longshoremen, especially as they grow older, have the prerogative of working less and shortening their work week, while still earning enough to get by comfortably. They have worked hard most of their lives and have come to believe this choice to be their right, a part of their way of life. They value this choice and will go to any extreme to protect and preserve it. And they do not feel that there is anything so terribly heinous in holding these values and passing them onto the next generation when those longshoremen come into the industry.

CHAPTER TWENTY-ONE

Caught in the Bight

The bight, pronounced *bite*, is something no longshoreman, seaman, or rigger should ever let himself be caught in. To visualize the bight, think of a baseball diamond. If you secure one end of a huge rubber band, say, or a rope or a steel cable, to first base, then stretch it across and anchor it firmly at third base, and then, with some strong mechanism, catch the center and stretch it all the way back to second base, you have placed the pitcher's mound in the bight. If the hold at second base is suddenly released the line will sweep up anyone standing on the pitcher's mound and fling that person toward home plate. If it doesn't cut him in two, that is.

Unquestionably, the bight is a dangerous place in which to be, and everyone who works around machinery where bights are created by rope or wire cable always cautions newcomers not to stand there. If a block or pulley gives way, you are liable to be caught in a lethal game of tag.

"Don't stand in the bight!" old-timers were always telling me when I first came on the waterfront. And then finally I became an old-timer and I got to say it: "Don't stand in the bight, damn it." Sometimes, if the newcomer repeatedly ignored the advice, I would, as was done to me, add the word "asshole."

The problem with all this is that sometimes it is impossible to stay out of the bight. The demands of the job may be such that one is compelled to place oneself in the bight to get the work done. A line gets twisted, a pulley flops over and is not feeding the cable correctly, or, as frequently happens, something jams for no reason at all. When that happens, someone has to step in and straighten it out. If you can stop the machinery—the pulling process—before stepping into the bight, you have minimized the risk. But work much of the time takes place in concert with other workers, and stopping the process is difficult or impossible to do. Also, a cable under tension may have more than one source pulling on it. All this is a preamble to explaining how this old-timer got caught in the bight. Was I an asshole? Probably.

When you work at potentially dangerous jobs, you expect to get hurt. You do not expect to get badly hurt, certainly not killed, of course, but you know that injuries come with the job; sooner or later they are going to occur, and it just might be your turn. Usually you can work through a sprain, a pulled muscle, a cut deep enough to be called a gash, but a serious injury, broken bones, for instance, can be a life changer.*

---

* This presupposes that you are not one of those people, and they are not all that rare, who look forward to an injury, hopefully minor, which they can trade for paid time off and, they hope, a future settlement of some kind of money, however small.

One of the most difficult ships to tie up that routinely comes into our port is a large vessel on which the cargo vans are driven aboard. Unlike the regular container ships where the vans are lifted off the chassis by a crane and deposited aboard ship, one on top of the other, these vans remain on their trailers, which are themselves lashed to the deck. When the vessel reaches its port of discharge, the tractor drivers come aboard, hook up to a trailer, and haul the vans down the ramps between decks and out a side port to the dock.

This vessel has four decks, and the top deck is a vast expanse of flat steel exposed to the weather. Indeed, when all the vans on their trailers have been driven off the top deck and it is bare, it looks like a flattop and looms above you on the dock like an aircraft carrier. Tying up the bow of this ship is especially difficult. The vessel uses one-inch-diameter wire cable, and the crewman paying out the cable is on the winches sixty feet across the top deck on the offshore side. We can't see him and he can't see us. Furthermore, the commands he gets to pay out, stop, or take up cable come from the bridge of the ship, 600 feet aft. Night or day, the winch-driver follows orders from the bridge; there is no bos'n or other crewman looking down on us signaling directions to him.

The last time I worked tying up this ship, it was two-thirty in the morning. It is a large vessel, calling for eight linesmen. Four were aft to tie up the stern, and three others and I were waiting at the bow. As the ship neared the dock, a crewman threw us a light heaving line, which we quickly grabbed and rapidly pulled in to get the larger hauling line to us as quickly as possible. Our first tie-up line was to be wire cable. We could see that the other end of our hauling line was tied to a big eye, a loop spliced into the wire cable. The eye of the wire was protruding from a hawse-hole just below the top deck of the ship. Before we four could get ourselves in place to begin hauling in the wire, we saw the eye followed by the rest of the cable drop rapidly out of the hawse-hole and straight down into the water. That wire weighed approximately ten pounds to the running foot. We were going to have to drag a couple of hundred feet of it across the bottom of the Bay. One of us, Owens, ran off to get a forklift truck to help us haul. We were going to need it.

When Owens returned, I made a bowline knot in the hauling line and secured it to the back of the forklift. We threw the hauling line over one horn of a steel double bollard, and Owens drove the lift away, slowly dragging the wire over the bottom until, covered with mud, it came up out of the Bay. Our plan, when the cable broke through the water, was to have Owens drag the loop at the end of the wire and about ten feet of the cable through the horns to give us some slack on the other side of the bollard. Owens would then stop and slowly back up so we three, Bobby, Charlie, and I, could throw the loop in the cable over both horns of the bollard, securing the ship to the dock. We three stood back, watching the moving cable and waiting until it was positioned where we could work it. I stood farther back on my side—Bobby and Charlie were opposite me— because the wire, as it came through the bollard, was turning at an angle, putting me in the bight. It was not an angle as severe as first, second, and third base, but it was an angle nevertheless, and one is automatically careful. Owens continued dragging the wire, stretched tight from its own weight, through the bollard until we had about the extra ten feet we needed, and we motioned him to stop. The three of us stepped up to grab the wire loop. The next thing I knew I was lying spread-eagle, flat on my back, about ten feet to the rear of where I had been standing. It happened that fast.

For some reason, lack of communication we guessed, the seaman who was paying out cable reversed his machinery and started reeling in. He tight-lined the wire so fast, it jumped the horn on my side of the bollard and, catching me mostly on the upper side of my right leg, picked me up and threw me backward. I was probably lucky. Three feet higher and it would have cut off my head.

When you are injured, if you are not unconscious, the first thing you think of is, *How bad?* Lying there on my back, I knew that I had caught one. After a little while I stood up. Then I took a step. Then I walked around in a small circle. That was a surprise. I felt a sense of relief. Maybe I had escaped the big one.

Charlie and Bobby came running over to me. "You okay?" Charlie asked. The cable, winging its way in my direction, had left them out of the line of fire.

"You all right?" Bobby asked. "Maybe you'd better sit down." I made another circle, to see if I could still do it.

"I'm okay," I said. "I can walk."

"Take it easy," Bobby said. "We'll pull the rest of the lines."

There were four more bowlines and a springline remaining to complete the job. I leaned up against a light pole and watched them finish tying up the ship. Then I limped off to fill out an accident report. Nine months later they replaced my right hip.

I did not know it when the accident happened, but my days of working were over. After my hip was replaced, I returned to the lines-board for one job. The gang had to carry me. I could not move fast, and, when I planted my feet to pull a line, my right leg would not accept enough weight to give me enough pull to make a difference. My life of work, which had started when I was barely fourteen years of age, had come to an end.

CHAPTER TWENTY-TWO

The Ghosts in the Factory

E. P. Thompson, in his landmark book, *The Making of the English Working Class,* records the confusion and despair of an entire people, evicted from their homes and run off their lands, their way of life destroyed by the Enclosure Laws or their cottage industries made superfluous by factories with power looms. Many of them migrated to Australia, America, Canada, and elsewhere. Those remaining stumbled around for two generations before coming together as a class once more in the mines and factories of a finally industrialized Britain. The factory and mine experience reconstituted them into labor, with an identification, loyalty, and common purpose that eventually led to a political party that, however much it may have failed them at times, ruled Britain in their name.

America's history is different, of course. Corporate farms, put together by big money and worked by big, expensive machines, created an enclosurement of their own with the result that mass migration to the city and factory became even greater than in Britain—less than three percent of Americans now make their living in agriculture. Unfortunately, for displaced Americans it never resulted in a labor party sizeable enough to gain power. Indeed, in earlier days the American Federation of Labor under the leadership of Samuel Gompers not only repudiated any attempt on the part of working people to become politically organized, but openly opposed Eugene V. Debs's efforts to do so.

The failure of American labor, unionized or not, to gain greater political power in the late nineteenth and twentieth century is remarkable since its achievements in other areas have been outstanding. Unquestionably the biggest threat to the world in the twentieth century was the emergence of Nazi Germany and Imperial Japan. It was a blue-collar America that created the overwhelming mass of war material that equipped our blue-collar military and our allies to defeat the Nazis in Europe. The victory in the Pacific was almost entirely an American effort. It may have been a peasant army that swept over China in the late 1940s, but it was an American blue-collar army and navy that defeated Imperial Japan and made that Chinese revolution possible. Without our strong presence, the world would certainly be a different place today.

The Bureau of Labor Statistics tells us that although union membership is now down to 14.5 million workers, over 112 million people classified as workers presently exist in this country. That includes everyone, blue collar, white collar, pink collar, all of us, anyone who does any kind of work for someone else that provides him or her with a weekly paycheck. This means that almost 100 million workers are alone out there, unrepresented by anyone other than themselves individually when they face the employer. So far this mass of people have yet to come together on common ground, identify with each other, and move to make a collective effort to better themselves both economically and politically. On the surface this enormous group would appear to be fertile ground for AFL-CIO organizing drives. To their credit the unions have been active among these workers, spending a lot of time, effort, and money trying to get them to join either existing local unions or new ones created for their benefit. Success has been achieved among schoolteachers and nurses, but after that their organizing efforts have been meager. Although the number of blue-collar workers has fallen dramatically during the last third of the past century, service workers have more than doubled. It is these workers who remain overwhelmingly unorganized. Service workers, although they are among the lowest paid in America, do not manifest much enthusiasm for joining trade unions. Everyone asks why—the unions cite high turnover of jobs, immigrants, and youths working part-time—but no one seems to have an answer.

It has been predicted, probably accurately, that industrial blue-collar workers are destined to continue to shrink in numbers. Continuously automated machinery requires fewer and fewer workers to turn out vastly more products. This is the fact of our lives. But as service workers have increased, their numbers have not impelled them toward organizing in the way blue-collar workers responded to the Industrial Revolution. A possible explanation may lie in that they have a workload but no product. Perhaps they see themselves differently. Does the act of merely serving others rob them of a sense of personal worth? The work they do is absolutely essential to maintaining a civilized world, but it goes largely unappreciated and, consequently, underpaid. Is it different working on an assembly line for General Motors turning out Chevrolets? Because the Chevys are there in the world and you helped build them, are you empowered in a different way to demand better wages and working conditions? All these questions are pertinent to the times and beg for answers.

Nurses and schoolteachers, however, are strongly organized. But they are skilled professionals with well-defined functions: restoring the ill to health and turning out educated kids. Both had affiliations before they had trade unions, and the simple experience of organizing themselves into a group may have led them inevitably toward creating a bargaining unit. The millions upon millions of service workers, however, seem unable to make the same collective move.

What of the 14 million workers still members of trade unions? Could they be the core of a successful resurgence of trade unionism and help organize the unorganized? Of course it is possible, but other factors have come into play. Unionized workers still plying their jobs in transportation, the building trades, and manufacturing make two to three times as much money as most service workers. They enjoy superior medical and dental care, vacations, and better pensions upon retirement. They still identify with their marginally employed blue-collar brothers and sisters who are eking out a bare existence on slightly more than minimum wages, but more and more they find themselves powerless to help them. In addition, the worker who borders on poverty can constitute a threat to the affluent job-holder; in the event of a strike they provide management with a huge pool of potential strikebreakers—scabs.

Although they are not widely publicized, wildcat strikes occur all the time. However, industrywide strikes appear to be happening less frequently, with modern American management shrewdly avoiding a confrontation they might lose. But the threat of scabbing out a strike is still there. West Coast longshoremen have not had to contend with scabs in the recent past, but in other aspects they are typical of the rest of labor. Their employers have found it cheaper to buy labor peace with high wages and then cut labor costs by farming out jobs or reducing them further through automation. With their numbers constantly decreasing, the principal concern of longshoremen and other organized workers making 50, 60, or 70,000 dollars a year is how to pass on their jobs to their sons and daughters. This makes them unlikely candidates for the future vanguard of the working class.

What will happen if the present trend in America continues? Despite a widely proclaimed decrease in crime, our prison population continues to rise. So crime, as it is presently defined, is really increasing and will very likely continue to do so. Apparently those whose choices are between a job paying seven or eight dollars an hour or living high off of selling narcotics prefer the latter, even with its risk of going to prison. Ironically, these people are fostering one of the few job categories showing an increase in America: prison guards.

If it has been a right-wing, laissez-faire philosophy that has brought us to where we are now, there does not appear to be a left-wing solution on the horizon capable of gaining acceptance and providing us with a classic socialist solution to our problems. Unfortunately, never, even in their most lucid moments of economic revelation, did either Marx or Engels, or for that matter anyone else, have even a hint of an insight into the direction industrialization could take itself under the control of capitalism.

What will America be like, what will it mean to America, if in the future it does not have a significant blue-collar working class? First, the working class is egalitarian and anti-elitist, so class stratification is likely to become more pronounced. Second, without a working class there will be no working-class neighborhoods, culture, or ethic, so these valuable pieces of America will be lost. The factory has not only created work, it has provided workers with a common existence and focus, both on the job and off wherever they gather together. The working-class bar, for instance, has not just been a hangout for drunks. Having a beer with your fellow workers at the end of the shift turns the bar into a staging area for everything from formulating a common position toward the boss to choosing up sides for the Saturday morning softball game. No one who has not been part of the social interactions present in a gathering of working men and women can understand the nuances of their conversations, the tacit agreements and conclusions they come to, or comprehend the process that brought the group together to act on an issue of common interest, whether it is to stage a slowdown, or decide who is going to play shortstop. This has been a significant part of the make-up of America. Now the working-class bar as an institution linking workers together is almost gone, and new industries, such as those in the various Silicon Valleys about the country, do not seem to be creating them or their equivalent. Losing blue-collar work is not only changing work, it is changing America.

Simple greed has never adequately explained those who use the means of production—the mines, farms, and factories—exclusively to further their own private motives and profit. Still less does greed describe these people when they compound their present damage by shipping whatever they can of the remaining jobs overseas. But for those workers who have been devastated by this dual loss, which in some parts of the Rust Belt has reached holocaustic proportions, it is maddening to observe the lack of concern by the rest of America for what was, and still is, happening all around them. No one word comes readily to mind to describe this deliberate destruction of a substantial part of the American blue-collar working class. Even more lacking is a vocabulary to describe those citizens who maintain that what is happening is good for our country. One hopes that when their history is finally written, some term can be found for them other than banal.

What can we do? It has been said that America is a collection of people in search of an ideology. If this is so, it is an unnecessary quest. We do not need an ideology to restore economic and social health to these displaced Americans. All that is required is to bring to these people that simple sense of justice and common decency that the vast majority of Americans already possess. If a more just America is to come about, however, the first question to be examined and put forth is *not* What is to be done?, but What we must *not* do, not do to each other? Something similar to the physician's credo: that is, "Do no economic harm."

It may come to pass that the blue-collar worker, the blue-collar culture, and the blue-collar ethic will no longer be a significant part of America. One hopes not. If the rewards of work, to the worker and to those who make use of the products of his labor, are subtracted from us, America will be the poorer. For us to keep this vital part of ourselves, work must be regarded as a right, and the right to work must be preserved. Having a job and doing necessary work is a primary need for everyone if they are to take their place in and become part of our society. All work, skilled and unskilled, must be preserved, justly rewarded, and shared as equally as possible. To increasing numbers of Americans, entering into the world of honest work is becoming less and less a possibility. Unfortunately, for them it is the only hope they have.

What will disappear from America as work goes? Countless things we will never know, or miss, or understand, until they are gone.

DATE			